M000119651

THE PRODUCT MANAGER'S GUIDE TO PRICING

BRIAN
WANLESS

Table of Contents

Introduction

This book has been written specifically for those who are selling products or services to consumers. While many of the examples in the book are drawn from consumer packaged goods, the principles and ideas discussed are applicable to any consumer product or service.

The intent is to help product managers and anyone else involved in making pricing decisions to make more effective and informed choices. Foremost it will provide you with the information you need to ask the right questions and search for the right answers. It will help you to understand information sources that are available to you and to use those sources more effectively. Hopefully it will help you to think about pricing in more innovative and strategic ways and find more effective pricing strategies.

Pricing as a discipline has progressed considerably over the past few years. Chief among the advances that have been made is the ability to measure and forecast the impact of pricing decisions. We no longer have to rely solely on gut feel or intuition as has so often been the case in the past. We now have the opportunity to make more informed and intelligent pricing decisions.

For consumer goods, the decision is made even more complex by the wide array of retail and distribution pricing strategies that have come to dominate the market. These vary from High-Low pricing to Every Day Low Pricing as well as regional pricing strategies. Long gone are the days when a product had one price chain wide. New channels have also created different price levels for a wide range of products.

In addition, the emergence of global retailers has created the need for global pricing that is attuned to different economies, competitive sets and consumers. Pricing strategies need to reflect this complicated and diverse reality.

For manufacturers or service providers, it means that pricing decisions have to take into account a myriad of possible price levels across diverse markets. Modeling these impacts and understanding how consumers will react to price changes is becoming more and more difficult every year. It requires not only a greater attention to detail but also a better understanding of the impact of price on consumer behavior.

This is not nor is it intended to be a comprehensive book on pricing. There are more pricing issues than I have addressed in this book that the reader can find in other books on the same subject. I have chosen to focus on those issues that are more commonly found when making pricing decisions at a product manager's or brand manager's level.

One apology or caveat I should add. Throughout the book I refer to `product` pricing and seldom `service` pricing. That is primarily for reasons of expediency. It is awkward to repeatedly use the phrase `product or service` and, therefore, I have chosen to refer to product pricing only. However, almost everything in this book that refers to product pricing applies to service pricing as well.

☆ ☆ ☆

The Importance of Pricing

Better pricing is one of the quickest and most effective methods to improve revenues and profits. There is almost nothing else you can do, no other management tool you have available to you that can have the same impact within the same period of time.

Despite the importance of pricing it is a management issue that is often neglected. Every year countless dollars in revenues and profits are lost due to poor pricing practices. We offer too many ineffective discounts, we under price or over price new products, we fail to raise prices when necessary, or we lower prices too quickly and unnecessarily.

There are few companies that can afford the cost of poor pricing. Today's profits are the driver of tomorrow's growth. If we leave money on the table we are starving our company of the fuel it needs to be competitive in the future.

For product managers, the importance of pricing is often personal. The success or failure of the products you manage, and ultimately your own performance, is measured in revenue and profits. Pricing can be the tool that helps you to outperform the category and competition. On the other hand, failure to deal with pricing can be an Achilles Heel that ultimately retards product growth and limits your career potential.

Why do we make so many poor pricing decisions? A common reason is because we fail to understand how prices work in the market place. Some of that failure begins with poor analytics. Too often we don't measure the impact that prices have on consumer behavior well enough to understand the impact of pricing. As a result we believe, erroneously, that our discounts are working, that we can't raise prices because the market is too price elastic, or that a price reduction will have positive benefits.

Some of the blame clearly belongs with the tyranny of anecdotal evidence. Our companies are rife with stories of purportedly negative pricing experiences. I was once told by a VP of Sales about a disastrous effort to eliminate coupons for toothbrushes and floss. Sales plummeted by almost 2%. What she didn't know, or didn't want to know, was that the cost of printing, delivering, and redeeming those coupons was equal to 5% of revenue, far more than the revenue and profit that they delivered. And yet her arguments prevailed and, rightly or wrongly, the coupons were reinstated.

Not all pricing stories are negative ones. Tales about the great pricing discount that drove sales through the roof are commonly told. They lead us to introduce even greater discounts and to do so more frequently. Too often these discounts are poorly analyzed and misunderstood. The lift we think we get is far less than what we actually achieve and too often at a cost that is prohibitive.

Much of the internal debate about pricing is driven by performance incentives that lead in turn to dysfunctional behavior. The demand for greater trade spending and more promotional events is often a function of the need for an account team or sales group to improve revenues at any cost. Other departments within the organization will have a different agenda. Finance, for example, plays the role of the defender of the bottom line. Their performance measure is tied to company profitability and, as a result, the Finance department is the first to argue for price increases whenever the cost of goods sold increases. Both of these positions can lead to inappropriate pricing actions.

Quite often we believe fervently that we can't change our pricing no matter how wrong we think it might be. We are slaves to our pricing history. We don't raise prices because we have never raised prices. We continue to discount because we have always discounted our prices. We believe that customers won't accept new pricing or changes to pricing in any shape or form. We have to line price. We need to have lower prices than our competitors. And so on and so on.

Now some of these beliefs that we currently hold might well be true. We don't know what is true or not until we are willing to question these assumptions and ask ourselves whether or not there is a better way forward. Failure to ask the right questions will almost undoubtedly lead to poor pricing decisions.

Fear of the unknown is another major deterrent to better pricing. Because we don't understand the impact of pricing changes, there is a tendency to believe that any change will result in a negative impact on revenue and profits. We need to be able to address those issues and prove that changes in pricing can result in both top line and bottom line improvements.

In many ways, better pricing is a result of more and better questions. If we ask the right questions and get the right answers to those questions we can begin to influence change within the organization. While this may sound self evident, it is by no means simple. In many cases the barriers to better pricing reside at the top of the organization. If senior managers do not understand the need for change or the opportunity that pricing represents, there is little need for others within the organization to do so. We need to challenge the status quo in order to find opportunities. One way we do so is by asking those questions that can lead others to understand that there is an opportunity gone missing.

One of the first and most important questions we need to ask is on what basis we make pricing decisions. How do we determine what is the right price for a product or service?

Value Based Pricing

There are three methodologies that are commonly used to price a product or service:

1. Cost Plus Pricing
2. Competitive Pricing
3. Value Based Pricing

Cost Plus Pricing is the practice of setting prices to meet a financial hurdle such as gross margin. It is, rather sadly, still used by many companies today. There are several drawbacks to using cost plus pricing, but the most damaging of all is that it bears no relationship whatsoever to the realities of the marketplace or what consumers are willing to pay. It may be nice to set a profit margin target of 80%, but if that margin results in a price that consumers consider to be too high then the product just won`t sell. And it can be all very well and good to demand a price increase to improve declining margins, but if the market reaction to a price increase is negative, then revenues and profit dollars will fall. This will often happen whenever prices cross a price threshold that results in a sizeable consumer reaction.

One of the principal benefits of setting a financial hurdle is that it acts as a safeguard that will ensure minimum profitability. But even this benefit has its unintended drawbacks. When we set a minimum profit hurdle we are unintentionally encouraging mangers to set a price that meets the hurdle and no more. But what if consumers were willing to pay a higher price? With cost plus pricing we never know the answer to that question. We could be setting prices too low.

Another common method for setting prices is to use a Competitive Pricing strategy. Competitive pricing is the practice of setting prices relative to a competitive benchmark. In some ways it's the lazy person's version of pricing (I'm too indifferent to figure out what the price should be so I'll rely on someone else to do it for me). It assumes first of all that your competitor has made a rational pricing decision which is not always the case. But even if they have and you do follow a competitor's pricing, it still begs the question as to what is the right relationship with that competitive product. Should your prices be slightly lower, the same, or slightly higher than the competitor's? How do you know which position optimizes revenue and profitability and what is the right difference in price?

Both of these methodologies can lead to under-pricing or over-pricing a product because both ignore the one primary question that is fundamental to good pricing – 'what are consumers willing to pay for it?'

Value Based Pricing is designed specifically to answer that question. Value Based Pricing means setting the price for the product based on the value that consumers place on it relative to other alternatives that are available to them. The concept of Value Based pricing suggests that if we can determine the value that consumers place on the product we can set the price in order to meet our objectives for revenue and profit. There is, of course, a lot more to setting prices than just measuring value, but this is and should be the starting point for good pricing.

Value Based Pricing incorporates the best attributes of both Cost Plus Pricing and Competitive Pricing. We always take into account the value relative **to competitive** offerings and, therefore, prices are set with competition in mind.

Value Based Pricing also directs us to design products with features that consumers are willing to pay for. As such, we only build in value that contributes to a higher price and margin and avoid those cost increases that have no value.

Another way of saying this is that we don't try to sell something to consumers at a price they are unwilling to pay.

With cost plus pricing we sometimes end up doing just that.

On the other hand, with Value Based Pricing we recognize that, in some cases, products have more value than is represented by their cost alone. As a result, we can actually obtain a higher margin for our product. This approach often results in higher margins and profitability, which is the same objective we are trying to achieve through Cost Plus Pricing.

✵ ✵ ✵

What is Value?

Value is the benefit that a consumer derives from a product or service. It consists of both tangible and intangible benefits, some of which we can measure and others that we cannot. But even though we cannot actually measure a benefit, we can measure how much consumers are willing to pay for it.

For most consumers value typically expresses itself in the Brand. A brand image connotes a range of different values to a consumer including effectiveness, trust, safety, and so on. Private label acetaminophen may be no different than a branded acetaminophen but for many consumers the brand provides a level of trust that just isn't there for a private label product (who knows what really goes into those products and whether they are safe to use). As a result, they are willing to pay a premium for the added value that the brand provides.

Brands also say something about the consumer who buys those brands and, by doing so, can fulfill a desire to express who and what we are. Nothing tells your friends, neighbors and colleagues that you are successful more than driving an over-priced sports car that you obviously don't need.   On the other hand, if you want to tell them you are a common-sense, practical person who knows the value of a dollar you might want to buy a fuel efficient mid-sized sedan.

In addition to the Brand, value manifests itself in the features that a product offers to consumers. Sun protection is a good example. Higher SPF ratings promise better protection from the sun's rays. The higher the level of protection the more benefit the product confers on users, the more they value the product, and the more they are willing to pay for that protection.

Price itself communicates value. If you know nothing about wine you can usually be sure that the higher the price the better the quality of the wine (not always true, but not a bad proxy). There are even some cases where raising the price of a product has resulted in higher sales volume due to an enhanced consumer perception of the value of the product. These instances are rare but they do happen.   On the other hand we know that, over time, if we under-price a product we will contribute towards a consumer perception that the brand has less value. It becomes a self-fulfilling prophecy.

When we measure what consumers value we are always measuring consumer perceptions of value and not actual value. Many aspects of value, including brand, are intangible and, as a result, are subjective in nature. Whether there is more actual 'value' in one product or another is a moot point if consumers believe it is true. As we noted earlier, branded goods almost always have more value than private label goods even when, as is sometimes the case, the two products are made by the same manufacturer with the same ingredients. As long as consumers *believe* that the branded product has more value, then for pricing purposes we can assume that it has more value.

On the other hand, just because the product has added features and benefits does not mean that it always has more value for consumers. Sony's Betamax was generally considered to be a better technology than VHS but for most consumers the difference was either unimportant or they placed more value in the idea that VHS was likely to become a more popular format for video rather than they did in the actual picture quality.

I cannot stress enough how important it is to focus on the consumers' perception of value rather than our own. It is very easy to get caught up in the internal hype surrounding products with features that have no value to consumers. At the same time, it is possible for consumers to see value where we see none. We need to understand what it is that consumers value about our products and services and base our prices on that perception of value, not our own.

✧ ✧ ✧

How Do We Measure Value?

The way that we measure a consumer's reaction to value and price (or how they trade off price and value) is through price elasticity. Simply put, price elasticity is a measure of the percentage change in volume for a percentage change in price. As prices rise or fall, consumers decide whether or not the price of the product represents better value than the alternatives available to them and, if it does, they switch to that product; if it represents worse value than the alternatives, they switch to another product or do without.

If we can measure price elasticity, we can model the impact that a price change will have on sales volume, revenue and profit. First we need a better understanding of price elasticity, what it is, and how we use it.

✧ ✧ ✧

Understanding Price Elasticity

Price elasticity and cross price elasticity for consumer products and services are two concepts that are often misunderstood. While in theory the concept of price elasticity is relatively basic, when we apply that concept to a market place we find that it becomes far more complicated. Price elasticity and cross price elasticity are constantly changing numbers that can vary significantly depending on a number of factors. In order to use these measurements properly we need to first understand what they are, how we measure them, and how to use them. The key is to identify *useful* price elasticity and cross price elasticity measurements.

In addition to price elasticity and cross price elasticity, we also need to calculate what I call Net Price Elasticity. As we shall see, this is the net effect of a price change across a portfolio of products, a concept that is highly valuable when dealing with consumer products and services.

Let's start with the basic definitions and then discuss some of the vagaries of price elasticity.

Definitions

Price elasticity is a measure of consumer reaction to a change in price. As prices increase consumers will as, a rule, buy less; as prices fall they will buy more. The extent to which they do so is called price elasticity. The formula for price elasticity is the percentage change in volume divided by the percentage change in price for any given product.

In addition to price elasticity, we need to understand cross price elasticity. Cross price elasticity is a measure of how much consumers will switch to some other product whenever prices are changed for a different product. For example, if P&G were to raise prices for Crest toothpaste by some amount and consumers switched from Crest to Colgate toothpaste, the extent to which they switched to Colgate would be measured as the cross price elasticity between Crest and Colgate. The formula for cross price elasticity is the percentage change in volume for Product A divided by the percentage change in price for Product B.

Price elasticity and cross price elasticity are quite often mirrors of each other. If there is high price elasticity for a product it is often true that there is high cross price elasticity with other products as well. This occurs because, in most cases, whenever a product loses a lot of volume due to a price increase, or gains volume due to a price reduction, it is either losing that volume or gaining it from another product. The more it gains or loses, the more the other product must gain or lose and, therefore, both price elasticity and cross price elasticity will be high.

There are some exceptions to this rule. In some cases consumption increases or decreases with changes in price and consequently it is possible to have high price elasticity for all products in a category with relatively low cross price elasticity. This is exactly what happened when prices for wireless phones and phone services decreased in the early years of that market. Lower prices enticed an entirely new set of consumers into the market for wireless phones. As a result, all companies experienced a growth in their sales and revenues. There was high price elasticity but relatively low cross price elasticity.

☆ ☆ ☆

Price Elasticity Depends on the Circumstances

While quite often we read about or see price elasticity numbers for a product or a category, in reality there is no such thing as a single 'price elasticity' or 'cross price elasticity' for a product. It is quite possible to get many different measures of price elasticity or cross price elasticity depending on the circumstances. These are not just small variations due to differences in measurement methodology. These can be very large differences that are dependent on how you measure it, where you measure it, and what you measure. These measurements will also vary depending upon which products are on the shelf, which way the price changes, competitive actions and reactions, and so on.

Price elasticity measurements also change over time. What you measured last year or two years ago might no longer be relevant today. Those changes are due to a number of factors such as changes in the economy, brand equity, competitive set, and your own products.

This variation in price elasticity has great implications for pricing strategy and the pricing decisions that we make. If consumers react differently depending upon what we offer and how we set prices, then we have the opportunity to find pricing situations that provide us with the optimum revenue and profit. Not all pricing options will have the same consumer impact. Some pricing changes could result in a loss of revenue while others could result in growth in revenues.

I cannot overemphasize the importance of this characteristic of price elasticity and consumer reaction to prices and I will come back to it later on. It is the basis for identifying and setting out a sound pricing strategy.

Here are some of the more important ways in which price elasticity changes depending upon the circumstances and how it affects consumer decisions.

✫ ✫ ✫

Price Elasticity Will Vary Depending Upon What is Available to Consumers

Consider a simple world in which there is only one product in one size. The price elasticity for that product is primarily a measure of the extent to which consumers are willing to do without it.

Now suppose that a second product is introduced by a competitor and that this product is very similar to the existing product. If consumers consider the two products to be reasonable substitutes for each other, then we would expect the price elasticity for the original product to change. This is because consumers now have two options: the first is to do without the product, while the second is to choose the second brand. More options equals more price elasticity (not always, but as a general rule of thumb it is true; it is possible that the second option could be so unattractive that it has no impact on consumer choice, but that would be a very rare occurrence indeed since it is unlikely that such an option would ever be presented to consumers in the first place.)

In addition to having more brands, flavors and competitors, price elasticity for any product or SKU will increase simply by virtue of having more *sizes* on the shelf for that product. If consumers have multiple sizes available for the same product (think 500 ML, 1 Liter and 1.5 Liter, for example) then a price change on any one size is likely to result in a greater shift in volume. Say, for example, that we raised the price on the 1 Liter bottle while keeping the price for the 500 ML and 1.5 Liter bottles the same. Consumers could react by switching to the 500 ML or the 1.5 Liter sizes if they were to perceive that these represented better value. If there was only a 1 Liter size available, consumers would have fewer alternatives.

This principal is important because not all retailers carry every product in the category. In some cases, the available products on the shelf will be few in nature while in others consumers will have a wide range of products from which to choose.

Let me give you an example how this works in practice. An analysis of the price elasticity and cross price elasticity of shampoo using historical data showed that for a particular brand there was no cross price elasticity between the 22 ounce and the 15 ounce sizes but there was high cross price elasticity between the 22 ounce and the 9 ounce size. At first glance this doesn't seem to make any sense. Why would consumers switch from a 22 ounce to a 9 ounce size and vice versa when they could switch to a 15 ounce size? But it does make sense when we realize that in many cases retailers in certain channels only stock the 22 ounce and the 9 ounce size. Consequently, the historical data found very little evidence of consumer switching to the 15 ounce size because the 15 ounce SKU was just not available to switch to in the channels that were measured.

What would have happened to price elasticity and cross price elasticity measurements if the 15 ounce size had been available to consumers? Quite likely there would have been higher price elasticity for the 22 ounce size because more consumers would have found a 15 ounce size to be a more attractive alternative than the 9 ounce size. Cross price elasticity for the 9 ounce size would be lower because consumers who did not like the price for the 22 ounce would have switched to the 15 ounce size instead.

Changes in the shelf set layout or design can also affect consumer decisions and price elasticity. Setting competing products against each other on the shelf is a good example of a change that will affect consumer behavior. Whenever we place competing products side by side we are in effect making it easier for consumers to compare products and prices. That often results in higher price elasticity.

When we measure price elasticity we have to be aware of what is on the shelf and how this will impact our measurements. It is quite possible to obtain measurements that vary considerably just because of the presence or absence of different SKUs in the shelf set. This is particularly true when we are using historical data to measure price elasticity but it also applies to survey methodologies as well. When we do this sort of measurement we also have to be aware that the measurements we get apply only to those shelf sets that contribute to the measurement. In cases where there is a 15 ounce shampoo on the shelf, for example, we will get a different measurement of cross price elasticity and of price elasticity. The measurement that we obtain in those cases will apply only to those shelf sets, and so on.

You might ask how we can reasonably be expected to identify every shelf set that exists in the market place. You can't and there are obviously some limitations to how far you can go in terms of specificity. But in most markets you can identify the ones that contribute the majority of the sales volume since these will be relatively few in number.

✽ ✽ ✽

Price Elasticity Changes as Prices Cross Thresholds

Consumer reaction to price will increase as prices cross key psychological thresholds.   One of the more common price thresholds that you might be familiar with is the $1 level.   In markets where products are priced at $0.99, any attempts to raise the price over $1 are typically met with a significant loss in volume.

Price thresholds appear at various price levels.   For products priced under $10, any one dollar price level is usually a key threshold.   The $5 and $10 thresholds might be even more important.   As prices increase, the importance of a single dollar threshold tends to diminish and consumers pay more attention to five dollar and ten dollar levels.   As prices go even higher, up into the $1,000 and above range, $100 and even $1,000 dollar price thresholds become more significant than lesser amounts.

When we measure price elasticity we have to be very careful to pay attention to these thresholds and the impact that crossing them has on volume.

What we find in practice is that the changes in volume when crossing a price threshold can have even more impact whenever there are other products on the shelf that are not crossing the same threshold.   When we take the concept that price elasticity varies due to different shelf sets and add to it the concept of price thresholds, we find that there is a cumulative impact on consumer behavior – price elasticity and cross price elasticity can be higher or lower for a given price threshold depending upon what else is on the shelf and whether or not these products cross a price threshold as well.

✳ ✳ ✳

Price Elasticity Varies Depending on Whether Price Goes Up or Down

Price elasticity can also vary dramatically depending upon whether it is a price increase that is being measured or a price decrease. This is particularly true for premium priced goods. A price *decrease* often means that the premium priced product is now within a price range that is acceptable to a much larger portion of the marketplace which has not previously purchased the product. As a result, it is quite possible that volume will increase substantially. A price *increase*, on the other hand, affects only those consumers currently buying the product. We can reasonably expect that this would result in lower price elasticity since there is some brand loyalty among existing consumers.

Any time there is a private label or low-priced brand in a category, we can expect to see the same sort of impacts from a price decrease. Most brands in the category will experience a volume lift from a price decrease because that brand is now attractive to all of those consumers who are normally buying a lower priced product with presumably less value.

When we measure price elasticity we need to separate measurements for price decreases from price increases. We also need to identify who is being affected by the price change and measure their price elasticity. For a price decrease, we want to know the impact on purchases for those who do not currently buy the product, but for a price increase we are more concerned about the impact on those who regularly buy the product. Both groups will have a different reaction and therefore we will get different measures of price elasticity.

Here is an example that illustrates the point. For a certain feminine hygiene product, the price elasticity for all consumers represents about -2. This means that if we were to change the price by about 5%, we would expect a volume shift of about 10%. For brand loyal consumers in this category, however, the price elasticity is only about -.7. This means that a 5% price shift for these consumers would result in a volume shift of 3.5%. If we were to consider a price decrease, we would most likely use the market elasticity of -2, but if we were considering a price increase we would choose the brand loyal price elasticity of -.7.

✵ ✵ ✵

Price Elasticity Measures are Unique to the Price Shift that is Measured

The formula for price elasticity is Percentage Change in Volume divided by Percentage Change in Price. When we measure or calculate price elasticity we arbitrarily choose which percentage change in price that we want to use. We need to be careful which one we choose because choosing different changes in price will result in different price elasticity measures. This is because price elasticity is not linear and can change particularly as prices cross thresholds. Here's a simple example to illustrate the point.

Suppose that we measured the volume shift for a price increase from $0.99 to $1.09. That is a 9.6% change in price ($0.10 divided by the average of $0.99 and $1.09). Let's assume for a moment that the volume loss in this case was equal to 15% (-15%). The calculated price elasticity would be -15% divided by 9.6% or -1.56.

Now let us consider a price increase from $0.99 to $1.29. The price increase is equal to 26% ($0.30 divided by the average of $0.99 and $1.29). Because the price elasticity between $1.09 and $1.29 is lower than it is from $0.99

to $1.09 the volume loss associated with the increase from $1.09 to $1.29 is lower as a percentage of the price increase. Let's assume in this case that we lose an additional 10% volume, for a total volume loss of 25%. The calculated price elasticity is now -25% divided by 26% or -.96.

Both numbers are correct measures of price elasticity. While I have made up the numbers in this case, in reality we often find that this type of situation exists.   As prices cross a threshold the volume loss is greatest around the price threshold and lessens as we raise prices further. This has implications for both how we measure price elasticity but also as to how we raise prices when we cross price thresholds.

Summary Table

	Price Shift A	Price Shift B
Original Price	$0.99	$0.99
Ending Price	$1.09	$1.29
% Price Shift	9.6%	26%
% Volume Shift	15%	25%
Price Elasticity	-1.56	-.96

For our purposes, when we talk about a price elasticity measurement we need to describe the measurement in terms of the actual price increase that is being discussed. Instead of saying that the price elasticity is say, -1.2, we need to say that is it -1.2 when we raise prices from $3.99 to $4.29, for example, and we recognize that the measurement would be different if we were talking about some other price change.

☆ ☆ ☆

Price Elasticity Depends on Competitive Reactions

Price elasticity will vary greatly depending on how prices are changed. If all competitors change price at the same time, the volume shift for each can quite often be very different than if one competitor alone changes prices. I have seen for one product, which shall remain nameless for confidentiality reasons, a price elasticity of -2 when only one brand raised prices and -.25 when prices were raised on all brands. For a 5% price change, this is a volume impact of either 10% or 1.25%, which is a very great difference indeed. It would be easy to argue for a price increase for this product if all competitors were inclined to raise prices, but very difficult, and probably ruinous, to support a price increase for one brand only.

This has very great implications for historical data analysis in particular. Most of the time, when we use historical data, we focus on the price shift for one product only. But if there have been shifts in competitive prices as well we can get a completely different measure of price elasticity.

✵ ✵ ✵

Price Elasticity Varies by Segment and Channel

Value and perceptions of value vary by consumer segment and the same is true of price elasticity. Brand loyal segments are much less price sensitive than those who are less brand loyal. Consumers who prefer a certain feature or benefit that a product delivers can often be less price sensitive than those who do not. When we measure price elasticity, we should always ask ourselves who is going to be affected by the price change. Will it affect all segments or just brand loyal consumers? If just brand loyal or feature loyal consumers, then shouldn't we measure their price elasticity only and not worry about others?

There is another implication to the fact that price elasticity varies by segment. In many categories, price promotions are common. Walk into any grocery store and you will see orange juice, cereal, soft drinks, and many other categories with some sort of price promotion each week. If a product is in a category that is heavily price promoted, then it is reasonable to ask whether or not list price has any impact on non-brand loyal consumers. They will purchase the product that is on sale. Therefore list price only matters for brand loyal consumers. We do not care about the list price elasticity for the non-loyal consumer since they hardly, if ever, buy our brand at list price. We care only for the list price elasticity for the loyal consumer. On the other hand, we do care about the promoted price elasticity for the non-loyal consumer since this is the one who will be affected whenever our product is on sale.

Finally, price elasticity will often vary by channel as well. There are a great many differences between retail channels that can affect price elasticity. Some merchandisers attract a more price sensitive consumer. Internet channels tend to get a high proportion of price sensitive shoppers who are more willing to search for a lower price. When we measure consumer reaction to prices, we need to be aware of how different channels react and which prices are appropriate in each one.

In some cases, we have the ability to segment products and prices by channel. In Club stores we can offer larger volumes and package sizes that are not available elsewhere. We should always assume that the reaction of consumers in these stores and channels will quite likely be different than that in other channels.

✲ ✲ ✲

Net Price Elasticity

As we have already noted most consumer products and services come in a variety of sizes, flavors, and features. As we create more offerings in our product line up, we will almost always find that price elasticity for each individual SKU increases. This should be intuitive. As consumers have more offerings from which to choose they are more likely to switch if they perceive that one product within the same brand is more attractive than another. This is partly because the brand, which is a huge driver of consumer selection, is a non-factor when choosing between products within the same brand.

Whenever we change prices within a portfolio of products we will get different volume shifts depending upon how the price relationship between products has changed. Some products in the portfolio might lose volume, while others might gain volume. Often the net gain or loss in volume across the portfolio is more important than the gain or loss in volume for any individual product. If we gain volume in one size or flavor, and lose it in another, but the net gain for both products is zero, we haven't really gained anything. Conversely, if we lose volume in one product but gain it all back in sales of another product we haven't lost anything.

In many cases when we consider prices and price changes, it is important to take into account these net gains or losses in volume rather than focus on the volume gains or losses of individual SKUs. Here's an example to illustrate this point. (All of the data for this example are available to anyone who has access to scanner data through any of the vendors offering this service.)

Monistat is a product used to treat vaginal yeast infections. It comes in a variety of formats including 1 Day, 3 Day and 7 Day treatments, as well as in creams or ovules and with added features such as cooling wipes. In 2006, key retailers raised the price of 1 Day Monistat. In many Drug stores, the retail price for some 1 Day products crossed the $20 price threshold while others did not. This resulted in a significant shift in volume from those where the price crossed $20 to those products where the price stayed under $20.

Here is the situation (I've simplified the product line up and pricing to make this easier to follow.)

1 Day Products	Original Price	New Price	Volume Shift
Monistat Day or Night	$19.99	$20.99	-10%
Monistat with Cream	$18.99	$19.99	+12%
Monistat	$17.99	$18.99	-5%

In this example, Monistat Day or Night lost a lot of volume as its price crossed the $20 price threshold. Almost all of this volume shifted to Monistat with Cream and the result was no loss in volume for the brand.

If we viewed this price increase focusing on Monistat Day or Night only we would probably conclude that it was an unmitigated disaster. However, if we look at the net gain or loss for the brand, we can see that it was quite successful (the weighted average price increase was approximately 4% with a 0% volume loss). The net price elasticity for the brand, we can argue, was zero.

✳ ✳ ✳

The Implications for Pricing

When we put all of these considerations together we find that there are many different ways in which consumers will react to prices. The range of their reaction can and often will be quite different depending upon how prices are set. Raising prices 5% across the board on all products will have a completely different outcome when compared to say raising prices selectively on some products and not others. Setting prices for one size higher or lower relative to another will have different impacts depending on which relationship we choose, which options consumers have available to them, which thresholds we cross or don't cross, how competitors react or choose to set their prices, and so on. Furthermore, these consumer reactions will differ from one market segment to another and from one channel to another.

Armed with this knowledge we can search for pricing relationships that result in higher revenues and profits than those that currently exist. We may also find that there are ways of raising prices that result in more revenue and profit than others. The benefits of doing so will become more evident when we discuss portfolio pricing strategy.

I cannot emphasize this last point enough. Creative pricing solutions are built upon an understanding that there is an optimum pricing relationship between products and that this relationship can and will change over time. We need to understand that as consumer reactions change we need to search for these relationships and adjust prices accordingly. It is seldom, if ever, as simple as just raising or lowering prices on all of our products. There are always alternatives that can and need to be explored.

These differences in how consumers react to prices have a real impact on how we measure price elasticity. We can get different price elasticity measurements depending on how we measure it and what we measure. All of these measures can be technically correct but not all of them are *useful*. The price elasticity measurements that are most useful are those that most closely resemble the circumstances that we are trying to achieve, whether that's a price increase or decrease, a price increase for one brand or all brands, a price increase for all products or just some products, and so on. It could be the price elasticity for a single product or the net price elasticity for a portfolio of products.

If we are going to optimize prices we need to search for and identify these relationships using price elasticity and cross price elasticity information that is relevant to current prices and future prices. That means we need to measure price elasticity and cross price elasticity, or in other words how consumers trade off price and value.

Measuring Price and Value

There are many ways that are commonly used to measure price elasticity for consumer products and services and it is important to understand the strengths and weaknesses of each. As we saw in the last chapter, we can derive many different measures of price elasticity depending upon what we measure and how we measure it. But not all of these measures are useful to our purposes. If we are going to find useful and relevant measures of price elasticity that will ultimately drive pricing decisions we need to engage in pricing analytics that are capable of providing us with measurements that fit the circumstances or pricing situations that we are considering.

Basically pricing research methodologies fall into two main camps: historical data and survey data. Historical data refers to actual sales data as measured by scanners or other methods of tracking sales in real time (commonly called POS or Scanner Data) as well as price tests. Survey data consists of any information gathered through a quantitative survey.

I will start with POS or Scanner data since that is one of the more common methods in use today for measuring price elasticity for consumer products.

✳ ✳ ✳

Scanner Data
Scanner data is a collection of unit sales volume by SKU. It is typically available from vendors such as IRI or AC Neilsen who collect POS data from various retailers. It is also sometimes available directly from retailers.

For many people the attraction of scanner data is that it measures real changes in price and volume. Because it is based on actual data, as opposed to a survey, the impact of factors such as brand loyalty that can affect sales volume are already built into the analysis. Unfortunately, lots of other factors are also baked into scanner data. Changes in advertising expenditure, changes in the shelf set, economic conditions, and bonus packages are just a few of the other factors that can affect sales volume. When we ignore these other factors we can't be sure whether the change in volume we see is solely a result of the change in price or whether it is due to something else.

One of the limitations of historical data is that it is relevant only to the specific circumstances in which it is measured. It does not apply to any other circumstance and cannot be extrapolated beyond the ranges that are actually measured.

In reality, using scanner data is a bit like driving a car by looking in a rear view mirror. It can tell you where you've been, but it's not a very good indication of where you're headed. This is particularly true if the pricing action that you are contemplating is set to cross a price point or threshold that you've never crossed before or enter into a pricing relationship that does not currently exist.

Let's take a look back at the Monistat example from the previous section. Any reading of the scanner data for 1 Day Monistat would have concluded that the price elasticity for Monistat Day or Night was quite high while for Monistat with Cream it was quite low (in reality, these products had a positive price elasticity because unit volume increased even though their price increased at the same time).

That analysis would be correct for this particular situation. But the price elasticity measurements would have been quite different if, for example, the prices for all of the 1 Day Monistat SKUs had crossed $20.   We cannot say looking at the scanner data what would happen in that situation.   Nor can we say that the volume loss for Monistat Day or Night would really be as high as it was had the price of Monistat with Cream crossed $20 or, for that matter, if Monistat with Cream was not available on the shelf.

These volume shifts are unique to this situation and this situation only. You cannot safely apply the lessons learned from this pricing action to any other situation or pricing change that differs in any meaningful way. That is the basic limitation of using scanner data to try and predict the impact of any future pricing change.

By extension, using scanner data to measure price elasticity has very limited uses. The price elasticity measurements that you get are justifiably accurate. But they have no implications for any pricing actions that you propose to take that are different than what has been measured historically. This is the key difference between just measuring price elasticity and measuring *relevant* price elasticity.

Another key limitation of historical data is that as circumstances change, the price elasticity measurements become quickly dated. As soon as new products have entered the category or new competitors have emerged, the shelf set has changed in any way, economic circumstances have changed, and so on, the price elasticity that you have measured from the past is no longer applicable. Of course, this is true of survey data as well.

✳ ✳ ✳

Price Testing

Another method for measuring price elasticity is to use a `price testing` methodology, sometimes called a 'test and

learn'. Price testing is a process of changing prices in a se-
lect market to observe how consumer behaviour changes
with different prices. Typically several markets are chosen
for the price test, with different retailers in each market
participating.

While the results of a well managed price test can provide good results, it is a very difficult process to manage.
For a test and learn methodology to be valid, the test markets need to reflect as much as possible the market place
in total. The retailers should represent all channels and
price levels, the consumer demographics should represent
the total market demographic, and the shelf sets should be
representative of the shelf sets that are seen in the total
market.

We should also be careful to take into account any
changes in the market place that can affect the test and
learn. The time period must be chosen so that seasonal
variations are eliminated. Shelf sets should not change during the test and learn. Advertising expenditures should be
consistent throughout the testing period.

We need to monitor and take into account competitive
behaviour during the test period. Any competitive product
launches, promotions, or other marketing behaviour could
alter the impact of the test results.

Test and learns can also be very expensive because it
is necessary to test only one pricing option at a time. The
results are valid for that pricing option only and should not
be transferred to any other pricing situations.

Price testing does work somewhat better whenever we
are testing different promotional prices. This is usually because promotional pricing is specific to individual retailers,
resellers or channels. The promotional price is tested in
all stores for that retailer or channel simultaneously so we

have a complete match with the market place demographics. In addition, promotional price periods are reasonably short in duration and, therefore, there is less chance of external interference in the price test. Nonetheless, all of the usual caveats apply. We need to be aware of competitive behaviour, changes in shelf set, seasonality, and so on that could affect the results.

There are further challenges for promotional pricing analysis that are discussed later on under Promotional Pricing.

☆ ☆ ☆

Discrete Choice Analysis

One of the more common survey methodologies for measuring price elasticity is Discrete Choice Analysis. This is a survey technique that is used to measure consumer response to different pricing scenarios.

In this type of survey a respondent is shown a series of offers at different prices. Based on the choices that the respondents make in the survey, we can measure how consumers trade off price against other features such as brand. From this data we can develop a simulator that can be used to then model different pricing scenarios.

The strength of Discrete Choice Analysis is that it enables us to test a wide variety of situations, even those that do not already exist. We can test the impact of crossing a price threshold that has not yet been crossed, the impact of competitive reactions to a price change even though those reactions have not yet happened, and the impact that a new product with different features or benefits can have on current volume. We can also test different sizes. In addition, we can determine the impact that different pricing relationships between SKUs will have on total volume for a brand when prices are raised on one size and not another, or on just part of the brand portfolio. In short, with this type of survey methodology we have a lot of flexibility to learn about a variety of different pricing situations.

The weakness of Discrete Choice Analysis is that it is a survey and like all surveys it is subject to error. Poor design can result in inaccurate results and it is possible to create survey designs that lead to nonsensical findings.

Two rules for surveys we should always follow: keep it simple and as much as possible reflect reality. It doesn't do us any good to give respondents situations that cannot exist in the marketplace.

Another challenge we face is the ability to include all products that are available to respondents in the survey. In some cases, there are so many different products available to consumers that it is impossible to show respondents every available option. In this case, decisions must be made to scale back on the options to make the survey practicable. While this can be done, we always run the risk of eliminating options that are meaningful to respondents.

✵ ✵ ✵

Simulated Shelf Set

Simulated Shelf Set is a survey technique that measures consumer response to changes in price for a complete set of products. The test is divided up in to several different groups of respondents. Each group of respondents is shown one shelf at one price level for all of the possible products on the shelf. Market share for each group and shelf set is tabulated and compared across all groups to determine the impact that price has on consumer choice.

For a simulated shelf set survey to provide a meaningful result, each group must be identical to every other group in the survey. If not, then the results for each group are likely to vary significantly. Identical groups should have the same demographic profile, represent the same channels, and have the same purchasing behaviour. By purchasing behaviour, we mean that the consumers in each group should have the same number of consumers for each SKU that is in the test. For example, if we had a test with only two products in it, then each group should have the same number of consumers buying product A and product B. If not, then we often get a result that shows significantly different purchases within each group.

The design of a simulated shelf set requires a good deal of management in order to get valid results. Like a price test, we can only test one pricing option at a time and this can become fairly expensive quite quickly.

☆ ☆ ☆

How much research and analysis is appropriate?

It depends upon the risk and rewards of the pricing decision. The larger the risk and the greater the reward, the more effort you should put into making sure that the pricing decision is the right one.

It doesn't make sense to argue over whether the price should be $3.89 or $3.99 or to spend a lot of effort to measure the price elasticity between these two prices. It is highly unlikely that the 10 cent difference would have any impact on volume. But it can be important to determine whether it should be say $4.99 or $5.09, especially if you believe or have some evidence that $5 is a price threshold.

I don't believe that any one method of measuring price elasticity is infallible. The more measurements you can take, the better and more accurate your measurements will be. Look for corroboration of research, historical data, or whatever other methods you are using to measure price elasticity.

Don`t be afraid to use your own judgment. If something doesn`t smell right, then it probably is wrong, even if everyone else vows up and down that the analysis was perfect in every way.

Tips for Price Elasticity Analysis

Here are some tips to follow whether you are using historical data or survey data to measure price elasticity.

If You Use Historical Data:

1. Identify current retail prices and determine whether or not your pricing action will cross previously uncrossed pricing thresholds. If it does, this analysis will not be of any use.

2. Pay attention to the shelf set. Limit the analysis to the current shelf set whenever possible.

3. Determine whether or not there were competitive price shifts at the same time as prices changed for your product that might affect sales volume.

4. Try to identify and eliminate other factors that will affect volume – shelf set changes (addition or subtraction of competitive products as well as changes in the layout of the shelf), changes in advertising expenditure, bonus packages, and competitive price shifts are just a few.

5. Separate price increase reactions from price decrease reactions in the analysis. A price decrease volume shift will not necessarily be the same as a price increase volume shift.

6. Separate price elasticity results by channel and price level.

If You Use A Survey:

1. Segment the survey by channel. Retail prices differ significantly by channel and the reaction to price often varies by channel as well. It is quite possible that prices will cross some thresholds in some channels but not in others and the survey needs to be able to measure those differences.

2. Model different shelf sets based on actual shelf sets in the market. Differences in shelf set will affect cross price elasticity and price elasticity.

3. Pay close attention to actual retail prices that exist in the market.

4. Use a broad range of prices in the survey. Anticipate where retail prices are likely to end up after a price change.

5. When modeling the results, eliminate sales volume that is sold on promotion. This will not be affected by list price changes and, if it is sizeable, could skew the results.

Understanding and measuring price elasticity is just the first step in pricing. Our next objective is to use that information to build a pricing strategy.

✲ ✲ ✲

Pricing Strategy

Pricing strategies come in many different shapes and forms. They can be as simple as 'We will have the lowest prices every day' or they can be intricate amalgamations of pricing policies and positions designed to support marketing strategy.

Whatever the strategy adopted, it should be something that can be condensed down to a few key principles that are easily understood and communicated to everyone.

While there are many different considerations that can be taken into account when creating a pricing strategy, for many it comes down to the basics – what is the optimum price for our products, can we change prices to increase revenue and profit, and can we sell our pricing strategy to our customers, whether those are consumers, retailers, distributors or some combination of all three.

In considering pricing alternatives, we must keep in mind several factors that will affect the outcomes. How will retailers or distributors handle any price change? Will the price change impact on distribution decisions – will retailers decide to change the product set that they carry? What will competitors do? What impact will a price change have on promotional pricing? How does the new price support and fit with other marketing objectives?

To answer these questions we need to broaden our horizons and put on our thinking caps. Here are the primary issues we need to consider when we develop a pricing strategy.

✷ ✷ ✷

Pricing Strategy Supports Marketing Strategy

The first and most important role of any pricing strategy is to support our marketing objectives for brand equity, market share, revenue, profitability and growth. In some cases, these objectives will apply to specific SKUs while in others it will apply to our overall portfolio of products within the category.

While this statement may appear self evident, in practice it can lead to quite different pricing policies. If, for example, the objective is to build market share, then pricing strategy will need to be one which gains new customers. As market share becomes stabilized and the cost of building market share grows prohibitive, the marketing objectives may change to one of maintaining share and building profit at which time the pricing strategy should change to follow suit.

These objectives can and often do vary by geography, segment, channel, and product. Where these differences occur, pricing strategy should be constructed to support the marketing objectives in each case.

It is almost impossible to build an effective pricing strategy without a clear marketing strategy with realistic objectives. If you can`t articulate your marketing strategy you have little hope of being able to do the same with your pricing strategy.

Quite often the inability to do so leads to a disjointed pricing strategy with no clear direction. This results in the sort of pricing where we have pricing policies that work against each other. For example, we have high list prices because we want to build profit and brand equity and lots of promotional pricing because we want to build market share. It is as if we can`t really decide what it is we want and therefore we try to be all things to all people.

Discount pricing and heavy promotional pricing are both inconsistent with marketing strategies that are built around high brand equity, high quality products and technological innovation. Low prices will communicate to consumers that the brand, the products and the innovation are of low value.

☆ ☆ ☆

Segmentation

One of the fundamental tenets of Value Based Pricing is that not all consumers share the same values. Take the example of sun care. Some consumers want or value a higher SPF rating while others will consider a higher rating to be excessive and of no incremental value. Still others might perceive that a high SPF rating is consistent with an oily or greasy feeling and would prefer to have a lower rating with a non-greasy feel. There are other features and benefits to consider as well. Some sun block treatments are waterproof, others are designed to stay on during physical activity, some are lotions while others are sprays. Each product and combination of benefits appeals to a different segment of consumers.

By segmenting the market according to value we can design and price products that appeal to each of these segments. We also optimize revenue and profitability because we are pricing each of these offerings for the segment that places the most value on those features and benefits.

In consumer products and services we often segment the market by using what is called 'self-segmentation'. With self-segmentation we let consumers segment themselves into different groups by offering them different product and value propositions at different price levels. Consumers then choose which product offering they value the most. Our challenge is to create the right assortment of offerings to properly segment the market and optimize our sales.

One of the more common failings in pricing strategy is the temptation to offer consumers added features and benefits with no increase in price in the hope that this will increase market share. There is a basic fallacy that underlies this argument. Those who value any added features or benefits will be willing to pay to get them. Those that don't will stick with what they have. Yes, some portion of the market can be persuaded to switch to a new product that has features or benefits that they don't really want just because they can get them anyway at the same price. But this is usually a small percentage and results in much less market share growth than we expect. (Think about it for a second – if they don't really value the feature, why would they switch brands even if it doesn't cost anything to do so? Remember that brand is also a key part of value and will likely have more importance for consumers than the feature. On the other hand, if they do value the feature they should be willing to pay for it.)

How much should we segment the market? The simple answer is as much as you can. However, there are some limitations to price segmentation. The size of each segment needs to be sufficiently large enough to warrant some differentiation in price. If the segments become too small we risk losing shelf space because retailers will not be able to carry every product. In addition the value differential between segments should be sufficiently large to justify the price difference. As we continue to segment the market, we often find that these differences are reduced to the point where they can become meaningless or impractical.

Market segmentation is also a very effective competitive strategy. By creating different product options at different price levels we can potentially isolate our competitors and limit their market share. The example of Crest Whitestrips is a good illustration of how this works.

Case Study: Crest Whitestrips

When P&G launched Crest Whitestrips the product came in one format. It was a 14 day treatment sold at one price, typically in the $29.99 range. Subsequent product launches introduced new innovation, starting with a more intensive treatment that required only 7 days, followed by a still more intensive treatment of only 5 days duration.

As new products were launched, P&G introduced new pricing tiers to the category. The price for the basic original product was lowered to $19.99 SRP. Newer products with added features and benefits were priced at $29.99 SRP and $34.99 SRP.

This strategy had a number of positive benefits. By stratifying the market pricing, P&G was able to increase category revenue and margin for both themselves and the retailer. The lower price point for the original product brought new users into the category. At the same time, the higher prices for the new products upgraded the sale for many existing users.

There was another side benefit to this strategy. By launching new innovation at different price points, P&G put pressure on other products in the category. From a retailer's perspective, it was of more value to put a new Crest Whitestrips product on the shelf at a higher price and margin than to keep an existing competitive product on the shelf that had a lower margin. Moreover, P&G's market share grew at the expense of its competition meaning that the inventory turnover and profit value of competitive products was decreasing.

Competitors who were limited to just one SKU in the category could not match P&G at each of the different price levels. By pricing each product at a different price level, P&G had effectively segmented the market leaving competitors to compete in only one segment while leaving the other segments to Crest Whitestrips.

Portfolio Pricing Strategy

Most, if not all, consumer products and services come in a variety of formats. For consumer packaged goods, there are multiple sizes, flavors, and features. For electronic goods there are different sizes, features and specifications. And we don't even want to get started on communications with its wide array of service plans, phones, and features.

As brands multiply their offerings, there is an interaction between different elements of the product line up. The market becomes further segmented as consumers sort themselves according to their preferences. And setting prices for each product or SKU within the brand becomes more complex.

Portfolio pricing strategy is the concept of setting the price for all of the products within a brand in order to optimize the revenue and profits for the brand. This differs from setting the price for each SKU within the brand separately in order to maximize the revenue and profit for each one individually. In essence, Portfolio Pricing Strategy says that the sum is greater than the total of the individual parts.

Value Base Pricing theory tells us that different products within the same brand will appeal to different segments of the market. Take Listerine mouthwash for example. The product comes in a variety of flavours and formats. There is the original Base product in three flavors, an Advanced formula that promises greater tartar control also in three flavors, and Listerine Whitening, all available in multiple sizes. Each of these products appeals to a different segment of the market. There are some consumers who are willing to pay for a Whitening benefit and others who will not. Some consumers will prefer to buy a large size while others prefer a smaller size. Some will want extra tartar protection while others won't. And within each product there is some loyalty to individual flavors.

On their own, each segment has a price where revenue and profit are optimized. You could set prices for each product based on the maximum revenue for that product alone.

However, the prices that we set for each SKU will have an impact on every other SKU in the brand. Price a large size too low and it will attract buyers who are purchasing a smaller size. Raise prices on Advanced Listerine and consumers will switch to the original Base product. Raise prices on one flavour and consumers will switch to another. Whatever price we choose for each SKU will affect the volume of some other SKU in the brand.

When we build a pricing strategy we need to take into account these impacts across the portfolio and understand how consumers will switch within the brand based upon the price relationship between SKUs. From what we have discussed earlier we know that these volume shifts will vary depending upon what the price relationship is between SKUs, what price changes we make, what is on the shelf, and how competitors respond to our price changes, among other things.

This knowledge opens up a myriad of opportunities when it comes to thinking about our pricing and the optimal price situation.

The point I want to make is that you have options and that these options can have quite different results depending on what you choose to do. It's a far different world from one which says 'raise your prices 5% across the board'. Now we can think specifically about the different alternatives available to us and how we use price to deliver a positive outcome.

As new products are added to the portfolio, the relationships change. This may represent an opportunity to increase revenue and profits by re-pricing the portfolio to make it more appealing to consumers as well as more competitive.

Case Study: The Monistat Experience

We have already seen in an earlier chapter on price elasticity the experience of Monistat. This example is also a wonderful illustration of how portfolio pricing works and how we can use that knowledge to optimize revenue.

The problem facing Monistat was that the $20 retail price represented a real barrier. A price increase from $19.99 to $20.99 would result in a significant loss in volume. However, there is also a high cross price elasticity between Monistat SKUs. As a result, almost all of the volume lost from those products crossing the $20 price threshold is scooped up by those products that are priced below $20.

Here is a simple analysis that illustrates the impact on revenue. I've added in percentage sales volume for each product at the original price and after the price change. Remember from our earlier example that total unit sales volume remained the same after the price shift.

Product	Original Price	% Sales	New Price	% Sales
Monistat Day or Night	$19.99	50%	$20.99	40%
Monistat with Cream	$18.99	25%	$19.99	30%
Monistat	$17.99	25%	$17.99	30%
Weighted Avg. Price	$19.25		$19.78	

After the price increase, sales volume shifted between different products within the portfolio. The new weighted average price is $19.78 which is an overall increase in price for the portfolio of almost 3%.

This example illustrates the value of viewing price from a portfolio perspective. On its own, we wouldn't raise the price of Monistat Day or Night over $20 because the huge volume impacts that arise. But when we look at it from the point of view of the overall brand, the price adjustment becomes positive and we can safely raise prices across a major price threshold.

When thinking about pricing a portfolio, here are some of the key questions you should ask.

1. Do we have the right price relationship between package sizes?

2. Have we captured the value of different features and benefits of different products in the portfolio?

3. Does the price for each product in the portfolio support our market objectives for that SKU?

4. Have we captured the right price-value relationships across our portfolio?

✵ ✵ ✵

Price Leadership

The concept of price leadership is one that many people find to be intimidating. That may be partly due to a lack of understanding of how the principle works in practice as well as inexperience in dealing with it.

What is a price leader? In the simplest terms it is the company that takes the lead in raising or lowering prices within the category. Typically this occurs whenever all competitors in the category are faced with rising costs (or it could be falling costs) and, as a result, some price change across the category is required. It is more prevalent in cases where there is relatively high price elasticity within the category so that a price change in either direction has a significant impact on unit volume. Because there is high price elasticity no one company can afford to unilaterally raise prices.

In most markets, any company can be a price leader. There are some exceptions to that rule. In the hotel industry it is typically up to the highest price hotels to raise prices first so that all those underneath can feel free to raise their prices. In some industries, such as the airline industry, it is standard practice for companies to take turns acting as the price leader.

There are clear advantages to acting as a price leader. If costs have increased, then taking the lead to increase costs and doing so quickly will restore profitability. Provided that competitors follow the price increase, the impact on unit volume will often be negligible.

There are risks as well. First and foremost among these is the risk that a competitor will not follow a price increase. But there are also steps that can be taken to minimize this risk. These include:

- Announcing the price change well in advance to give competitors time to react as well as to allow time to rescind the price increase if competitors show no inclination to follow; and

- Making the terms and conditions of the price change flexible so that you have the opportunity to match competitors with respect to amount and timing of the price change.

The flip side of price leadership is price followship (if there is such a word). If faced with a similar situation, but unable or unwilling to take the lead, it is important to follow any competitive price changes as quickly as possible. There is often a temptation to take advantage of a competitive price shift to steal market share in the short run. This might not be a bad idea if you have a very low market share and competitors can safely ignore your actions. But if you have a sizeable share and do not follow there is always a risk that competitors will rescind the price change. Not only that but any future price changes will be made that much more difficult by your actions.

Remember that if **not** following a competitive price shift is valuable to your business, then doing so must be equally detrimental to a competitor's business. As a result, it would be profitable for that competitor to take back the price change if possible. When that happens, it's usually a lose-lose situation for everyone involved.

There is an exception to this rule. If your brand has a particularly small market share in a category where there are several sizeable competitors, then your decision to follow or not follow a price change will have little impact on competitive behaviour. In this instance you can most likely take advantage of high price elasticity to increase your market share and revenues.

Price leadership is applicable to both price increases and price decreases. In some markets, prices for legacy products are constantly being reduced as new technologies are introduced and the cost of manufacturing decreases. A responsible price leader in this type of market is one that recognizes when these price reductions result in the sort of results that benefit the industry as a whole. Typically this includes an expansion of the market as lower prices attract new customers who had previously not purchased these products. Another benefit is the reduction in inventory that is fast becoming obsolete.

When wireless phones were first introduced into the market place, the price of a phone and service was prohibitive to many consumers. But as price leaders reduced their prices, the market grew exponentially. The growth in sales volume for all manufacturers and service providers resulted in a substantial growth in revenue and profit. This is an excellent example of how price leadership downward can be a smart pricing strategy. But if you are going to consider this strategy please be certain that the market will grow.

While we typically think of price leadership in terms of list price, we should also consider this concept with respect to promotional pricing as well. We should be aware that our actions with respect to discounts and promotions can influence competitive behaviour, either positively or negatively. I will discuss this in more detail in the chapter under promotional pricing.

Competitive Response

Volume impacts will differ considerably depending upon competitive reactions. It is critical to understand how competitors are likely to react.

How competitors respond to a pricing action will also depend on their current situation and what impact the pricing action has on their revenues, profits and competitive position. Some of the key questions you should ask are:

- What is the competitor's current position in the marketplace? Which do they need more – revenue and profit or market share? How strong is their position on the shelf or with consumers?

- How does your competitor compete? Are they driven by brand equity and marketing, or are they focused on market share?

- What is their plant capacity? If a competitor has considerable excess capacity, it is likely that a volume increase would have more benefit than a price increase.

- How have competitors behaved in the past? Have they followed previous price changes or ignored them?

Other clues about competitive intentions can often be found in publicly available sources. It is not uncommon, for example, for a CEO to muse aloud to investors about the company's position on price and whether or not price changes are in the offing.

Line Pricing

Line pricing is the practice of setting the price for a range of products in the portfolio at the same price. In many ways line pricing is the antithesis of portfolio pricing. While one strategy seeks to diversify pricing the other tries to maintain one price across all products.

The principal arguments in favor of line pricing are:

- Promotional efficiency: the cost of buying down the retail price of a product on sale is less if all products are priced the same.

- Simplicity: one price for a range of products simplifies pricing on the shelf and makes it less confusing for shoppers.

- Optimized revenue: varying the price beyond the price threshold that the line price represents would result in a loss of revenue and profit.

Of all these arguments, only the last one is a valid reason for adopting a line pricing strategy. This is a case where the category has a significant price threshold that cannot be crossed and doing so would result in a loss of revenue. In this case, variations in product size have a more positive impact than changing price and, therefore, it makes sense to maintain the price at one level rather than setting different prices.

When line pricing does make sense it is usually because the differences between SKUs (other than size) are relatively minor and, as a result, consumers are indifferent to one SKU or another and will typically choose the lower priced option. Another way of saying this is that we cannot justify a price differential based on consumer value.

Line pricing solely for the purpose of promotional effectiveness can lead to a loss in net revenue and profits. For most products, the total annual sales volume sold on a promotion will be less than that sold at list price (if it is not, then you should seriously re-examine your pricing strategy). This is increasingly true in today's markets where EDLP retailers and resellers account for more sales volume. While EDLP retailers do offer price promotions these tend to occur less often than in high-low pricing channels.

Here is an example to illustrate the economics of line pricing for a typical consumer product. In this case, we will assume that our brand has two products on the shelf. Total weekly sales at list price average 1,000 units, 500 for each SKU, and that promoted sales volume is equal to 3,000 units. Every day retail price is $3.99 and the promoted price is $2.99. We will also assume that one of the SKUs (we'll call it SKU B) can be priced at a premium of $4.99. At this higher price we will assume that the sales volume for SKU B will fall to 400 units, while sales for SKU A will rise to 550 units, and the balance of 50 units of volume is lost to competitive products. This is an arbitrary assumption but one that would be most likely to occur if we are considering the proposition of differentiating the price between these products. It would make no sense to differentiate the price if consumers were likely to leave the brand were we to do so.

We will also assume that there are six promotional events per year for these two SKUs. The average cost to the manufacturer to buy down the price of the product is

$0.75. This would rise to $1.75 for SKU B if it is premium priced at $4.99. Let's compare revenues in each scenario.

	Line Pricing	Differentiated Pricing
Units Sold at list (46 weeks)		
SKU A	23,000	25,300
SKU B	23,000	18,400
Retail Revenue		
SKU A	$91,770	$100,947
SKU B	$91,770	$91,816
Total Revenue	$183,540	$192,763
Manufacturer's Price		
SKU A	$2.79	$2.79
SKU B	$2.79	$3.49
Manufacturer's Revenue		
SKU A	$64,170	$70,587
SKU B	$64,170	$64,216
Total Revenue	$128,340	$134,803
Manufacturer's Profit (assumes 70% profit margin)		
SKU A	$44,919	$49,410
SKU B	$44,919	$48,815
Total Profit	$89,838	$98,225

Note: the profit for SKU B is now $0.70 higher when priced at a premium, which is the difference between the selling price of $3.49 and $2.79.

Differentiated pricing results in a profit increase of approximately 9% over line pricing. Next we have to deduct the additional cost of promotional expenditure from our profit increase to arrive at the net profit increase.

Promotional Impacts
Units Sold on Promotion

SKU A	9,000	9,000
SKU B	9,000	9,000

Note: when the two items are sold at the same promotional price we assume that the sales volume for each one will be the same just as they were when sold at the same list price. This may not be the case in reality. Quite often when a product with premium features and benefits is sold at the same promoted price as another product in the same brand, sales of the premium product will be higher because consumers will perceive that it is better value at the same price.

Manufacturer's Promotional Revenue

SKU A	$25,110	$25,110
SKU B	$25,110	$31,410
Total Revenue	$50,220	$56,520

Manufacturer's Profit Before Buy Down

SKU A	$17,577	$17,577
SKU B	$17,577	$23,877
Total Profit Before Buy Down	$35,154	$41,454

Cost of Buy Down

SKU A	$6,750	$6,750
SKU B	$6,750	$15,750
Total Buy Down	$13,500	$22,500

Total Manufacturer's Revenue	$178,560	$191,323
Total Manufacturer's Profit before Buy Down	$124,992	$139,679
Total Profit After Buy Down	$111,492	$117,179

In this example differentiated pricing results in an increase in revenue and profit at all levels. Net profit in this case increased by about 5%. Of course, every situation will vary and many of the assumptions I've used in this case might not occur in reality. But we do have the ability to measure these results and determine what the actual difference will be. In most cases, differentiated pricing will result in higher revenues and profits when compared with line pricing. But don't take my word for it. Do the analysis yourself and ask whether or not line pricing is suitable for your portfolio.

☆ ☆ ☆

The Soft Price Increase

A soft price increase is a reduction in the size or quantity of product offered with no change in price. Effectively the price per unit of quantity increases while the absolute price remains the same. It is generally used whenever we believe that increasing the price would have a negative impact while decreasing the quantity would result in a positive impact, usually higher profits.

Confectionary products have been using the soft price increase for many years now. The $1 price threshold for candy bars, chewing gum and other products is often a significant barrier to any form of price increase. As costs of production have increased, manufacturers have chosen to reduce the size of the product rather than risk raising the price over $1.

When we consider a soft price increase, we need to be aware of how consumers will react to a size reduction. Their reaction will vary depending upon whether or not the change in size crosses a size threshold. Just like price thresholds, there are points at which the impact on consumer behavior will be significant.

For example, reducing the size of a candy bar from 56 grams to 50 grams, or from 8 ounces to 6 ounces, might not engender a consumer response. But if we were to reduce the size below 50 grams, we might find that consumers perceive that the quantity they are buying is much lower than before. As a result, a reasonable number of them might switch to something else.

One of the advantages of a soft price increase is the potential benefit on inventory turns. Fewer ounces or fewer units in a product should result in a shorter buying cycle. Provided that consumers continue to use the product at the same rate we would expect that they have to repeat their purchase more often. These higher inventory turns can have a significant impact on revenues and profits.

An impact on inventory turns is more likely to occur with products that are necessities or used by consumers at a constant rate. Some examples might be toothpaste, shampoo, and laundry detergent. We would not expect consumption to decrease just because the consumer purchased a smaller quantity. The same might not be the case with products where consumption typically varies with purchase volume. Potato chips come to mind as one product where buying less would probably mean less consumption with little or lower impact on inventory turns.

At the same time we have to be aware of brand loyalty. The inventory turn impact on revenue and profit will be greater if consumers are inclined to stick with the same brand over time. Products with very low brand loyalty are unlikely to gain much benefit from inventory turn increases.

The soft price increase and higher inventory turns are of some benefit to retailers as well and this should not go unnoticed. Retailers typically measure performance on the basis of inventory turns. A higher turnover usually means greater profit per square foot of shelf space. That can help boost a product's performance on the shelf and make it a more attractive proposition for the retailer. This is an important consideration in a world where products are fighting for shelf space.

☆ ☆ ☆

The Impact on Brand Equity

The price that we set for a product has a great deal of influence on consumer perceptions of value. Whenever we charge a premium for a new feature or benefit we are establishing in the consumer's mind the concept that this feature has value. On the other hand, when we don't charge for it, we are sending a clear signal that the feature has no value.

Over time, lower prices and aggressive discount pricing will erode brand equity. Higher prices might not always lead to perceptions of greater brand equity, but they are definitely essential in supporting any claims to better quality. I once heard of a museum that decided to charge an admission fee in order to cover its costs. Admission had previously been free. Unexpectedly attendance increased once they added an admission fee. Most likely consumers perceived that a museum with an admission fee represented more value than one that was free and, therefore, was worthy of their time. In this case, the price of admission clearly communicated the value of the museum.

The same rules apply to promotional pricing. In the long run, too many price promotions will erode brand equity. The brand becomes known as a 'sale' brand that can always be bought on sale somewhere. The sale price becomes the de facto list price and acts much the same as a permanent price reduction.

It is true that over time brand equities change and, as a result, pricing strategy must keep pace. This is one of those chicken and egg questions in marketing. Do we raise prices in anticipation of brand equity or do we wait until we have measured a change in brand equity, then adjust the price? The answer to this question depends on the direction of brand equity. It if is increasing, then price should be set in anticipation of future increases to brand equity so as to support the increase in equity. If it is decreasing then, price adjustments should lag brand equity so as to maintain whatever equity there is as long as possible, recognizing that ultimately some price adjustment might be required to reflect the future brand equity position.

☆ ☆ ☆

Bundling

In some consumer categories, bundling products or services together is a common strategy. Telecom companies typically bundle services and products together in various rate plans. Cable television companies bundle channels into program packages. Fast food chains create bundles of meals.

First and foremost it is important to realize that bundling is a form of discounting. The price paid for a package of products and services will always be lower than the total price for the product or service bought separately. And because bundles are usually permanent offers the price discount is fixed.

Because it is a form of discounting, the benefits arising from the bundle should exceed the cost of the bundle.

In other words, the volume lift that we get from offering the bundle should be greater than the price discount we offer.

Many of the basic pricing principles that we have already discussed apply to bundling strategy. When we create bundles we should consider the value that the bundle offers to different market segments, how consumers will react to the bundle at different price points, how the bundle fits with our marketing strategy, what the competitive response is likely to be, and so on.

One of the key principles of bundling anything is that all of the elements should have some value for the customer, or that consumers are at worst indifferent to the elements of the bundle. If, however, there is any part of the bundle that is unattractive to consumers, the bundle will fail.

There are two situations where bundles are successful.

1. Where the sale of all products in the bundle is higher as a result of bundling (lift exceeds discount); and

2. Where the bundle enables one competitor to pre-empt the competition.

The classic upgrade bundle is the McDonald's meal deal. While I never actually saw the results of any research, I have been told by a reasonably reliable source that McDonald's analysis showed that a lot of customers would order a sandwich (McDonald's lingo for any burger) and a drink, but seldom the fries, hence the oft asked 'would you like fries with that'. The bundle was meant to upgrade consumers to all three products.

This type of bundle works well whenever there is an element of the offer that is rarely purchased but is something that still has value for customers. Fries evidently fall into that category.

The pre-emptive bundle is one that is put together to foil the competition because they don't offer all of the pieces of the bundle. In what seems like a long time ago, Microsoft was the only software company that offered word processing (Microsoft Word), a spreadsheet (Microsoft Excel) and a presentation software (Microsoft Powerpoint). Their competitors were spread among separate companies such as Lotus 1-2-3 (spreadsheet software), and Harvard Graphics (presentation software). Microsoft was the first company to offer a bundle called Microsoft Office that combined all three products in one package that competitors couldn't offer.

Customers who wanted all three software products and compatibility opted for the Microsoft bundle. Competitors were too slow and too late to realize that they too needed a bundle in order to compete. The bundle effectively shut out the competition from a segment of the market that preferred compatibility between all three software products over anything else. The rest, as they say, is history.

✲ ✲ ✲

Promotional Pricing

Promotional pricing strategy, which is the subject of the next chapter since it really deserves a chapter onto itself, is and should be a subset of the overall pricing strategy. Just like pricing strategy, it must be consistent with our marketing objectives. Having a premium pricing strategy is inconsistent with having a deep discount promotional pricing strategy. The negative impact of promotional prices on brand equity will offset the positive impact of a high list price.

✲ ✲ ✲

Managing Prices

Pricing strategy is about more than making a pricing decision. There are other considerations as well that you should consider. This is by no means an exhaustive list, but these are some of the issues you need to take into account.

How Often Should We Make Pricing Decisions?

In most organizations some pricing decisions are being made all of the time. Promotional pricing is one of those constant decisions that are made each year and will often change over the course of each business cycle.

List price decisions are typically made less often, although in a global market where there are inflationary pressures and exchange rate issues, these decisions may require more constant attention. In some sectors, such as electronics and telecommunications, list pricing decisions are constantly being made as new technologies supersede older ones resulting in price adjustments.

I personally believe that pricing is a question that should be revisited often if not constantly. We seldom have perfect pricing, whether it is list pricing or promotional pricing. That means that there is always an opportunity to improve what we are doing.

Pricing should be a part of your business planning process every year, even if you are not making any major changes to pricing. You should at least be asking whether or not there are issues to be addressed and have an answer as to why you are not doing anything about pricing in that year.

Pricing Communications

Good communications are an essential part of pricing. We need to communicate both internally and externally to explain our pricing strategy, to justify our pricing actions and to influence future decisions.

Having a clearly communicable strategy is one part of good pricing communications. It enables us to explain the path forward and that ultimately will lead to more consistent pricing decisions.

Customer communications are equally important. A clear justification for a pricing action will make it much easier to sell to customers who might otherwise oppose any changes to price.

There are two ways to justify a price increase:

1. Due to cost increases; and

2. Because the value proposition justifies a price increase.

Using a cost increase as a justification for a price increase is anathema to some pricing experts because it flies in the face of the value based pricing model. Nonetheless, it has proven to be in many cases a very effective rationale for a price increase, particularly in cases where the customer has to absorb the price increase and cannot pass it along.

The distinct advantage of using a value based proposition as a justification for a price increase is that it is consistent with the selling message. This type of message is effective whenever you are delivering superior value relative to price and can increase prices while still delivering better or equal value than competitors. It is also effective whenever the price increase results in a win-win proposition for the customer, typically a retailer or distributor who will also benefit from higher prices.

Which is More Effective – Small Annual Price Increases or One Big Price Increase?

There are two schools of thought when it comes to price increases. Some argue that it is best to raise prices consistently every year by a small amount. Others argue that it is more practical to raise prices by a larger amount but less often.

The arguments for a small annual price increase are based on the notion that costs are increasing each year and that delaying a price increase will only erode profits until such time as prices are finally increased. Furthermore, a small increase of 2 or 3 per cent has the advantage of being relatively innocuous. It can be easily justified as inflation driven and therefore doesn't receive the sort of push back from customers or retailers that a larger price increase engenders.

If price increases are cost based, then there is an argument for matching the price increase to the cost increase. It is more difficult to justify a price increase based on past increases in cost especially if these have occurred more than two or three years in the past. There is some risk that if costs are not recovered quickly enough that they will be lost forever.

On the other hand raising prices in small increments can have serious drawbacks. Most small price increases will result in a retail price that is just slightly above a price threshold. In many cases this could result in a loss of revenue if price elasticity around the price threshold is high. Margin creep presents another problem. Retailers might be inclined to raise prices to the next threshold regardless of the price increase and, as a result, the manufacturer receives only a portion of the actual retail price increase.

Both the sales force and customers can tire of repeated price increases. The sales force dislikes having to approach customers each year with yet another price increase. If customers complain loudly enough there is always the potential for some rebellion against future price increases.

The right methodology will depend on the situation. If there are concerns about price thresholds and margin creep, it is best to avoid small annual increases in price and opt for periodic larger price increases. If cost inflation is persistent and significant then annual price increases might be warranted.

Anticipate Retailer Reactions

How retailers or resellers react to pricing is extremely important since it is the retailer or reseller who ultimately sets consumer prices which in turn are the prices that affect sales volume. When considering retailer reactions, you need to think like a retailer. Here are some of the key questions that a retailer will likely ask regarding a price change.

- What will other retailers do – pass it along or absorb the price change? If retailers think that their competitors will absorb the price change, they are likely to follow suit.

- What is the current margin on these products? How does it compare to the category average for the category? Does it meet or exceed the target margin for the category that the retailer has set. If the margin is low, you might expect retailers to take advantage of a price change to increase their margin.

- What are the expected category impacts? How important is this brand to the category? Do we need to be price competitive with this brand in order to build store traffic?

- How important is this brand to our retail customer, the consumer? Is it a good fit with our retail strategy at this price?

- How does the price change affect the shelf mix? Does it make these SKUs unique relative to other products already on the shelf?

- What impact would a price change have on store brands? Will they become more or less competitive?

Quite naturally, retailers want and expect to have a positive outcome from any pricing change. The most likely reaction from a retailer is the one that results in higher revenue and profit for the category and the store at the end of the day.

This applies to all merchandising decisions, including whether or not they will de-list the product. Sometimes the threat to de-list or remove support from a brand is used to dissuade the brand manager from making a pricing change, particularly a price increase. It's one of the tactics that account teams often use when they believe that a price increase is not in their best interests. While there is no definitive answer to this question, we can address the issue by assessing the likely impact of the price increase on the retailer. If the likely impact of the pricing change is positive, or if de-listing is likely to have a negative impact, then we should conclude that the threat to de-list can be dismissed.

✵ ✵ ✵

Consumer Reaction to Pricing

When we create a pricing strategy we need to be aware of how consumers will react to pricing. It's not just a question of price level. In some instances there are other factors that will influence consumer behavior. Three of the more common reactions include Price Thresholds, the `Good Enough` syndrome, and Pricing Policy Dissonance.

Price Thresholds

Many people find it difficult to accept the proposition that large numbers of consumers will switch for what is a relatively small price differential. After all, the difference between $1.01 and $0.99 is only two cents. Surely we believe that consumers are smart enough to recognize the difference in actual price is small. In reality, the vast majority of them are. The number of consumers who are switching when prices cross a price threshold is often a small minority of the total market but that minority nonetheless has a major impact on our decisions.

Here's an example to illustrate the point. Suppose we have a product priced at $2.99 and we raise prices by 3%. The new retail price is now $3.09. If price elasticity is high, say -2, then we will lose 6% of our sales volume. This means that 6% of consumers currently buying our product actually reacted to the price threshold. That is quite a small part of the total market. Nonetheless it is sufficient to result in a total loss of revenue and most likely a loss of profit as well.

There are several possible reasons why consumers react to a price threshold. It could be because some consumers focus on price from right to left. They see a difference between $2 and $3 and are not paying attention to the cents. It could be because the price threshold represents a barrier that they will not cross in that category (as in 'I would never pay more than $30,000 for a car' or 'I would never pay more than $10 for a bottle of wine'). For practical purposes, the actual reason doesn't matter. It is sufficient to know that the reaction exists. Having said that, if we know why consumers react the way they do it is useful in helping us to understand the reaction and explain the pricing reality to skeptics.

At the same time, once thresholds have been crossed consumer reaction to further price increases tends to mitigate. We find therefore that as we raise prices from say $3.09 to the next price threshold that price elasticity is lower, i.e. we are losing less sales volume relative to the price increase. This is one reason why, when raising prices, we tend to see that larger price increases are more effective in the short run.

We need to pay a lot of attention to price thresholds when pricing for consumers, both for list price as well as promotional prices. If you want to find a quick and easy revenue bump from pricing one of the simplest ways is to look at current retail prices to find those that are not at a price threshold and adjust those prices so that they are.

More recently, some price thresholds in some channels have disappeared or become less relevant. In the Dollar channel, where many products are priced $1, $2, or $3, consumers have become more accustomed to thinking that the dollar price level represents the best value. In these stores, a price of $1 might be just as effective as $0.99, although I have seen evidence that in some categories there is still a reaction to a price difference of one cent, even in the Dollar channel.

Wal Mart has also conditioned consumers to believe that prices below the obvious threshold (say $2.94 versus $2.99) are better value. I have seen some research that suggests for loyal Wal Mart shoppers that they react to $2.99 the same way that they react to $3.00. For these consumers the price threshold might be anything above $2.94.

We should never take price thresholds for granted, but in the absence of any evidence one way or the other, the safe bet would be that whenever prices cross a likely threshold that there will be a sizeable consumer reaction.

The 'Good Enough' Syndrome

The 'Good Enough' syndrome states that at some point the added value of additional innovation becomes meaningless to consumers. Typically this occurs with technological benefits where the added value of a technical feature is more than what consumers demand.

The Internet provides a perfect example of this argument. For many consumers, use of the Internet is limited to e-mail and web browsing. The downloading and uploading speeds required to process these applications are relatively low. For these consumers, higher speeds are redundant. They just don't need to receive their e-mails any faster.

On the other hand, there are segments of internet users, gamers for example, who will value faster download speeds and will be willing to pay a premium for that feature. But even these demands for speed, at some point, will be met by technology with the result that very few, if any, will demand higher speeds.

The Good Enough syndrome has implications both for pricing as well as product development. Just because we build it faster, stronger, clearer, or whatever, does not mean that consumers will be willing to pay a premium. We cannot charge a higher price for features and technologies that exceed the 'good enough' level.

As we build in more features, we need to identify which segments will benefit from the added capability and to what extent they will pay for it. If there is no value to the additional capability, we should question whether we need to build it in, especially if it means additional cost.

Pricing Policy Dissonance

Several years ago a television cable company decided it would be a good idea to introduce something called 'negative option billing'. Essentially the company gave a new service to all of its subscribers and added the fee for the service to the regular monthly bill. It was up to subscribers to call the company to notify them that they didn't want the new service otherwise they would get it along with the bill.

We don't know if the company deliberately made it difficult to cancel the service or whether they just did not anticipate that large numbers of customers would not want it. I tend to think it was probably the latter because someone most likely argued that the majority of consumers, when required to take action to stop a service, will be disinclined to do so. They were wrong. The phone lines were jammed and customers were furious.

The memory of negative option billing did not go away. Years afterward consumers were still angry and, in focus groups, it was the first thing that popped up when this company's name was mentioned. The impact of that policy didn't end when the policy was discontinued. It affected consumer decisions far into the future as the company launched new products and services. Competitors benefited from negative consumer perceptions that persisted for years.

It wasn't just the difficulty of cancellation that generated fury. Most consumers were upset by the mere flagrancy of the policy. They did not like the idea of someone foisting a product upon them without asking whether they wanted it or not.

It is a perfect example of how pricing policies and structures can create consumer dissonance. We can create the same sort of dissonance in other ways. Some of the more common examples include forcing consumers to take a bundle that they don't want, adding in hidden fees that only appear after the sale, or creating impossibly complex pricing plans that no one understands.

We engage in these sorts of pricing policies because, in the short run, they can boost sales and revenue. Ultimately, however, these types of pricing policies will create a negative backlash among consumers that will erode any goodwill that we have created and result in lower future sales. We need to understand the impact that our pricing policies will have on consumer perceptions of the brand or of our company and avoid the temptation to take advantage of consumers in the short run.

☆ ☆ ☆

Pricing with Imperfect Information

So far for the most part I have been inferring that whenever we make pricing decisions that we have information available to us as to how consumers will react to prices, specifically price elasticity and cross price elasticity measurements. Unfortunately this is not always the case. In some instances it is impossible to obtain reliable information on consume reaction through either historical data or surveys. Sometimes the market is too small to justify the expense required to do so while in other cases it is just impractical to try to survey consumers. For some industries, such as electronics and communications, the pace of technological development is such that price elasticity data is quickly out of date. As new products are launched the impacts of price on legacy products changes such that historical data or even recent surveys can become irrelevant and trying to measure the impact of each successive price change can become a nightmare in futility.

Whatever the reason, there will be occasions when we must make pricing decisions with imperfect information, if any information at all. I want to stress before I go any further with this section that I always recommend gathering information about consumers and consumer reaction to price whenever and wherever possible. I do not like `gut feel` or instinct when it comes to pricing because my experience tells me that these are very poor substitutes for information and quite often wrong. Therefore I strongly advise that what I am about to suggest to you should only be considered when it is impossible to do the homework necessary to get reliable pricing information.

Using Soft Information

Even though we might not have quantitative data as to how consumers will react to prices, we can often make inferences from qualitative sources. For example, while we might not know how consumers will react to a specific price for a new product with new features, we can gain some insight if we know how they view that product, the brand and those features. Market surveys, if available, can often be a good source of information as to how consumers view the category and various competitors. This type of information can give us some notions of value and whether or not consumers are likely to be price sensitive which, in turn, can be helpful.

Let Strategy Guide Your Decisions

Many of the concepts we have previously discussed with respect to pricing strategy can help in making pricing decisions even when we don't know the impact of price on consumer behaviour. The impact on brand equity, competitive behaviour, and channel response are all issues that can guide us when making a pricing decision in the absence of price elasticity data. Pay attention to these issues and they will inform your decision-making in a positive way. If your pricing decisions are consistent with the overall marketing strategy for the product and the brand it is likely that these decisions will be the right ones in the long run even if, in the short, they are not optimal.

Pay Attention to Thresholds

We know that consumer reaction to price increases as we cross price thresholds, but tends to decrease as we move upwards from those thresholds. If we don't know exactly where those thresholds are then we have to assume that anything that looks like a threshold will be one. If we have to cross price thresholds, then it makes sense to do so in a large way. It will probably be more effective, for example, to raise prices from $3.99 to $4.29 rather than to $4.09 because most of the unit volume lost due to the price increase would be felt when prices cross the $4 price threshold. Similarly if we are in a segment where prices are being lowered, such as consumer electronics, then we should look for price thresholds whenever we lower our prices. Rather than lower the price of an HDTV from say $1,049 to $1,029, we should probably lower the price to $999 because the increase in volume when crossing the $1,000 price threshold would have more beneficial impact on revenue and profit than the smaller price reduction.

Let Cross Price Elasticity Be Your Friend

Anytime we have a large number of different SKUs available for consumers we have a reasonable expectation that there will be high cross price elasticity between these SKUs. If that is the case, then we can take advantage of cross price elasticity to make pricing changes with much less risk. However, it is important to note that just because there are many SKUs in the category that cross price elasticity within the brand might not be high. I know of categories where there are many different SKUS but cross price elasticity is low. This is because consumers in these categories are more loyal to product features and package size than they are to brand. But these are exceptions and generally occur whenever the products within the brand have significantly different features. In most categories consumers will switch within the brand whenever prices are raised or lowered for any one SKU within that brand or category.

If we are forced to raise prices due to cost increases, for example, then raising prices on some portion of the portfolio will tend to carry less risk than raising prices across the entire portfolio. It is often less risky to take a large price increase or price decrease on one part of the product portfolio and none on the other parts of the portfolio. This is because by doing so we give consumers who are price sensitive an opportunity to stay with our brand without absorbing a price increase.

We should also look for opportunities to split our product portfolio with respect to prices whenever possible. This might mean taking products that are currently line priced and changing the price for some of those products but not others. This price segmentation takes advantage of cross price elasticity between SKUs to raise prices on some products resulting in a limited loss of volume relative to the price increase.

Backwards Analysis

A very useful analysis to undertake is one which asks what does the price elasticity and cross price elasticity have to be in order to make a price change successful. In this type of analysis we model the potential impacts of a price change then calculate what the price elasticity and cross price elasticity would have to be in order to break even. We then ask whether or not there is a reasonable expectation that the actual price elasticity and cross price elasticity are within range of the breakeven point. Of course we don't know what the real numbers are, but it the required price elasticity and cross price elasticity are either outside of the norms that we might expect for consumer goods and services then we can probably safely rule out any pricing changes.

Without information on how consumers will react to prices we can never be certain that any changes that we make will be successful. The best we can do is to use the knowledge that we have about how consumers react in general and try to use that to our advantage. But that is still a far better approach than one which simply raises or lowers prices across the board or blindly changes prices with no thought given to what the impacts might be.

✺ ✺ ✺

Service Pricing

For the most part, strategic considerations for services are very similar to those for products. Competitive reaction, segmentation, equity impacts and so on apply equally to services as they do to products.

Where services differ primarily is in the area of shelf life. While a product can sit on a shelf and be sold in the future if it is not sold today, if a service goes unused or is not purchased, the revenue opportunity is lost forever. If a seat on an airplane is empty, there is no way to capture revenue from that seat. If a hotel room is unoccupied, the revenue for that period is lost. And if a telephone service is unused, we can't go back in time and sell it to someone.

Because of this difference, pricing strategy for services must take into account the opportunity cost of pricing and how prices affect sales today and tomorrow. There are different methods for doing so. Revenue maximizing software is often used by transportation companies to monitor sales and adjust prices accordingly in order to maximize revenue for each trip. Depending upon whether the trip is oversold or undersold, prices might increase or decrease as the departure date nears in order to take advantage of consumer demand.

We don't always need sophisticated software to make these kinds of pricing decisions, although for a large enterprise such as an airline it is probably necessary. One company I know of uses a spreadsheet to estimate its capacity utilization on a monthly basis and adjust prices depending upon whether or not they expect utilization to rise or fall that month.   It is an effective, low cost methodology for making pricing decisions on the fly.

Because of the non-existent shelf life of a service, we commonly find discounts used as a method for increasing sales particularly during non-peak periods or times of economic uncertainty.   All of the rules for promotional pricing that I will discuss in the chapter on Promotional Pricing should apply to discounting for services as well. Price thresholds matter. Competitive reactions are important. Analysis of the net impact of the promotion is critical.

For some services, promotions and discounts can impact on future sales. A travel company, for example, that offers a discount for travel during a non-peak period could entice a consumer who might have purchased during a peak period. Provided that there are no vacancies during the peak period, this might not matter. But if there is excess capacity during the peak season, then we need to take into account the cannibalization that is occurring with the discounts.

Using Segmentation to Price Services

The principal of market segmentation is a key aspect of pricing services. As we discussed earlier under price elasticity, not all segments of the market place the same value on services. Some are more price sensitive than others and will react more to changes in list price as well as pricing promotions. These more price sensitive consumers will also tend to be more likely to adjust their use of services to take advantage of lower prices.

In many cases price sensitive consumers are more willing to trade off features and benefits for price.   This can manifest itself in many ways provided that prices are set in order to reflect different price sensitivities of different segments. One of the more common methods of doing so is to vary list price by timing. For most services there are peak periods of demand when most consumers want to take purchase. For travel services there are peak seasons when travellers prefer to visit certain destinations. For communications services there are times of the day or week when consumers are more likely to use the service. Sports teams have determined that there are certain games where the seats are more likely to be sold out. In each of these cases, it is possible to charge a premium.

At the other end of the spectrum, we find there are non-peak periods of demand. These include the off-season for travel, weekends for communications, and certain games where the attraction of the visiting team is diminished. During these periods, we can use pricing to encourage attendance for those segments of the market that are more price sensitive. These consumers will trade off the value that peak period represents for a lower price during a non-peak period.

Consumers can be segmented by more than just period of demand. Consumers will react differently depending on what the service incorporates. We have the option of creating a la carte services as well as packages and bundles. I won't repeat all of the rules about bundling because these have been covered in another section. The same rules apply equally to products and services. The point I wish to make here is that, much like we saw with portfolio pricing for products, we can do the same for services, creating different combinations of service options built around timing and features. How consumers will react to these different options will depend upon what we create. Our job is to find the optimum combination of price segments that will lead to the maximum revenue and profit. These will change over time as new services are introduced and, as a result, we must adapt pricing to ever changing circumstances.

For services, one of the benefits of segmentation is that is can create increased attendance or usage of these services. Consumers who would otherwise not be willing to use the service or attend the event because of price can be given offers that suit their budget. The result is a larger market for that particular service. We must, at the same time, be aware of the cannibalization impacts of pricing. Market expansion should not come at the expense of overall revenues and profits, unless of course attendance and usage are the primary goals or sales targets.

The more we can develop different pricing tiers and options for consumers the more we enable each segment to find the right price-value proposition. As with product pricing, there are limits to how many segments we can create. If we create too many pricing segments, we run the risk that the marginal impact of each segment diminishes to the point where it is negligible. In addition, we can create confusion among consumers which can result in a negative backlash in demand.

✡ ✡ ✡

Pricing in a Global Market

Global pricing strategy, like all pricing strategy, should be based on the concept that consumer values differ from one market to the next, from one segment to the next. This disparity in value is driven by differences in brand equity, competitive sets, and ability to pay, among other things. Culture can also play a role in shifting consumer values.

There are three key challenges facing any brand manager with respect to global pricing in today's market place:

1. Setting prices to optimize revenue and profit by market;

2. Pricing for multinational retailers operating in multiple markets; and

3. Reducing diversion or grey market activity.

All three of these are linked together. If not for multinational retailers and grey market activity the task of setting prices in each market would be relatively simple. I say 'relatively' because all of the other issues in pricing that we have already discussed still have to be dealt with and, as we've seen, those are not always simple.

Nonetheless both the emergence of multinational retailers and the increased ability of re-sellers to sell across markets create an added layer of complexity.

✷ ✷ ✷

Setting Prices to Optimize Revenue and Profit by Market

No two markets are ever alike. There will always be variances in distribution, brand equity, competitive sets, consumer incomes, and so on. Because of these differences, consumers will react to price differently in each market. Even within these markets, consumer segments may react differently than they do in other markets and we might find that the segmentation we use in one market is not suitable for another.

We should therefore approach pricing in each market individually and set prices based on how consumers will re-act to prices in each one.   The first step in this procedure is to identify differences in consumer value where these ex-ist (basically understanding how consumers react to price through price elasticity and cross price elasticity measure-ments).   Once we understand those differences we can proceed to establish a global pricing strategy for the brand based on those differences.

Still we need to be aware of cross market influences when developing a pricing strategy. We cannot ignore the issues of product diversion, multi-market retailers, and cur-rency flucations among others.

There is no simple and quick answer with respect to what the strategy will or should look like. Here are some of the key issues you will need to consider:

- At what price differential will product diversion occur? How does this vary by geography? Diversion profitability is linked to shipping costs and, therefore, it is obvious that the further away two markets are from each other, the greater the potential price disparity can be before diversion becomes profitable. Cost of shipping is also a factor.   The higher the cost of transportation, the less likely diversion will occur.

- Are there options to differentiate the product or service across markets to justify the difference in price? For example, is it possible to offer different warranties in different markets, to provide service options to enhance value in one market and not another, or to create different bundles? Can we link product strategy with pricing strategy in each market by, for example, limiting distribution of premium products to higher value markets, or creating lower cost options for price sensitive markets?

- Should we adjust the price differential by market region on only part of the product portfolio? For example, we could adopt a global floor price for low value products while maintaining separate prices for premium value products within our product portfolio. This might be feasible if we find that demand for some part of the portfolio, say the premium value products, is limited to a few markets.

Pricing in a changing global market will require constant adjustment. Growing economies create differences in consumer values that will require adjustments in prices. A long term pricing strategy needs to anticipate the rate of change and plan for price shifts accordingly.

✵ ✵ ✵

Multi-Market Retailers

The issue of multi-market retailers is a growing problem for brand managers. These retailers have the ability to monitor the price they pay for products globally. Once they spot a lower price in one market, they tend to want the same price in all markets, regardless of the price they charge in those markets.

If we want or expect retail prices to vary by market, we should also expect our prices to reflect those variations.

Consequently, our ideal strategy would have distinct prices in each market. How can we achieve this if retailers demand one price globally?

We do so by getting ahead of the curve and communicating our pricing strategy. Retailers are well aware that different markets require different retail prices. Our challenge is to communicate to retailers why our prices have to match their pricing in each market. We can do this if we have developed a global pricing strategy that reflects all markets in which we operate.

We can then argue that we have established an average global price for our products that is designed to help the retailer to penetrate each market in which they operate. This essentially means that while we have different prices in each market, the retailer should view our pricing in aggregate form – we have a global price that is based on the average price for our products across all markets. Our key message is that we make less money in some markets than others, but that is to be expected if we want to be successful in those markets. By doing so we are helping the retailer to be more competitive in those markets as well. The emphasis should always be on communicating that you as the manufacturer are earning less than desired in these markets, rather than having to explain why you are making more money in markets where your product is higher priced. It changes the nature of the discussion in a very meaningful way.

The key is to be prepared for this discussion beforehand. If you wait until the retailer or distributor raises the point, you will have more difficulty in making your case.

☆ ☆ ☆

Currency Fluctuations

Another common issue in global pricing is the impact that fluctuations in currency exchange rates have on prices. These are the rules of thumb when dealing with exchange rates:

1. Ignore short term fluctuations. For the most part, these have little or no impact on consumer perceptions of value or the competitive landscape. As a result, any change in price should have negative consequences (assuming that your prices are already optimized in that market.)

2. Where persistent inflation exists change prices quickly and often. All of the basic rules of pricing apply here. Pay attention to price thresholds in particular and move prices to each new threshold as quickly as possible. Be a good price leader or follower, whichever the case might be.

3. Look for opportunities to use changes in the exchange rate to improve pricing in that market. You can use these fluctuations to raise or lower prices if necessary to achieve the optimum pricing structure where you have evidence that prices are not optimized already.

✫ ✫ ✫

Global Floor Pricing

One of the ways in which companies try to protect prices globally is by applying a global floor price. This strategy is designed to maintain a minimum price level in all markets. It reduces diversion or grey market activity while establishing minimum margins.

The concept of a global floor price is very similar to cost plus pricing. The price itself has nothing to do with the market conditions in each market and, therefore, risks being either under or over-priced.

In practice, floor prices tend to act like a magnet that pulls all prices down to that level regardless of the price that might be charged in each market. Quite often there is pressure to set this price low enough to be competitive in emerging markets, or markets where the brand's equity is lower. There is then a tendency (a very strong one) to use this price in all markets, even those where a price premium might be had.

Global floor pricing might make sense where the threat of diversion is very high. In that case, the purpose of the pricing strategy would be to limit diversion. However, unless diversion is the key factor driving the pricing strategy it makes more sense to set prices in each market relative to those market conditions. It is still possible to have a global floor price, although its impact would be minimal.

✲ ✲ ✲

Promotional Pricing Strategy

Too often product managers overlook promotional pricing. They leave the details up to the sales force to implement and trust that they will use trade spending dollars wisely. This is not always the case and product managers should be more diligent in understanding the return on investment that they receive from trade spending or other promotional investments.

Promotional pricing is a common practice in the sale of consumer products and services. There are many different types of promotional prices the most common of which include coupons, bundles, retail price discounts, reward programs and rebates.

The use of promotional pricing can be justified as long as it meets either of the following criteria:

- It helps us to meet our marketing objectives for revenue and profit;

- It is necessary to maintain shelf presence, i.e. the retailer will not stock the brand unless the manufacturer offers promotional pricing.

The first of these objectives is deliberately phrased. Many will argue that promotional pricing most often results in an increase in revenue and profit. But in reality, promotional pricing very seldom if ever does so. This is because the unit volume lift for the promotion is seldom large enough to offset the price discount that has to be given to all consumers during the promotional event.

Many people working in a consumer product or service industry will likely dispute what I have just said. I am sure that there are many promotional events which, on the surface, appear to increase revenue and profit. But in most cases, this conclusion is drawn from a cursory analysis of the data. A more thorough analysis would probably indicate that the event resulted in lower revenue and profit *in the long run.*

Having said that, for many retailers, promotional pricing is a core part of their business strategy and, therefore, they expect manufacturers to provide trade funding to support this pricing strategy.   Since we have to live with promotional pricing, we might as well make the best of it.   We can start by at least making sure that we understand the impact of promotional pricing for both ourselves and the retailer.

Promotional Pricing Analysis

At a basic level, promotional pricing analysis should assess the impact of the promotion on net revenue and profit. The formula for this is simply the increase in revenue and gross margin dollars less the cost of the promotion. This equation can be stated in two parts: Promotional Revenue minus Base Revenue and Promotional Profit minus Base Profit. Base Revenue and Profit is the revenue and profit we normally achieve in any time period when the product is not on promotion.

When we calculate Base Revenue and Profit we should use an average for a period both prior to and following the promotional event.   Provided that sales revenues are stable during this period, we typically only need 3 or 4 weeks of non-promoted sales volume on either side to get a reasonably reliable estimate of base revenue and profit. There are some instances of weekly variations in sales volumes that we should be aware of that can affect the calculation.

However, this level of analysis is only the beginning. Promotional pricing impacts are often much more complex than this.

A more thorough promotional pricing analysis should take into account the following:

- Shifts in unit volume prior to and following the promotional event. In many categories, there will be a decline in sales both prior to and after the event. This can be created by advertising the event (consumers delay purchase knowing that a sale is coming) as well as by stocking up (consumers make advanced purchases while the sale is on). There are two elements of stocking up behavior that need to be considered: pantry loading and the forward pull of future sales volume. The formula for the analysis would now be adjusted by subtracting any sales volume declines in the week prior to the event and after the event from the promotional lift.

- Pantry loading. In many categories, pantry loading during a promotional event is commonplace. When consumers have every expectation that they will purchase and use the product in the future, they have an incentive to stock up on the product in question. Pantry loading activity will vary with the promotional event. The better the offer for the consumer the more they will purchase and stock up. Pantry loading is not typically an issue with consumables such as potato chips or chocolate. Consumers have shown that the more of these they purchase, the more they consume. But for many other items, such as shampoo, toothpaste, paper towels, and household cleaners, for example, consumption does not increase with purchase. These categories in particular need to be concerned about the pantry loading impacts of promotions.

• When we analyze a promotion that is susceptible to pantry loading we should take into account the effect of the promotional event on future sales. If pantry loaded has occurred then we should calculate the lost revenue profit from future sales and deduct this amount from the revenue and profit that has occurred. The formula for the analysis would then become: Promotional revenue and profit minus base revenue and profit minus lost future revenue and profit.

• The long term impact of the promotion. For categories such as consumer durables the long term impact of promotional events needs to be taken into account. Deep discounts or rebates can pull future sales forward resulting in a short term increase in volume followed by a long term (and by long term I mean over the next one to two years) decline in volume unless the promotions are repeated.

• Cross channel impacts. Some very aggressive price promotions can shift volume from one channel or retailer to another. This volume shift should be seen as a loss of revenue at list price and not an increase in overall volume. When analyzing promotional effectiveness it is important to look at total volume across all retailers.

• The impact of synergy. Some promotional events are timed to coincide with other marketing tools. For example, it is not uncommon to increase advertising around a promotional event, or to distribute coupons in support of the event. The impact of these additional expenses should be factored into the analysis.

- Long term impacts on consumer behavior. The repeated use of promotional pricing within a category will cause consumers to modify their behavior to take advantage of a sale event. We should pay attention to the impact that our promotions are having on consumer behavior to determine if, over time, we are shifting more and more volume to promotional pricing. (Quite frankly it is surprising to me that consumers ever pay list price for anything given that it is possible to buy almost everything on sale and that these sale events happen so often. The fact that they do pay list price can only be chalked up to indifference, laziness or poor planning.)

When we take into account all of these factors, the formula for analyzing a promotional event becomes the following:

Promotional Revenue and Profit − (Base Revenue and Profit) − (Lost Revenue and Profit in the weeks before and after the event) − (Lost Revenue and Profit due to Pantry Loading) − (Lost Revenue and Profit from future sales pulled forward) − (Revenue and Profit lost at other retailers or channels) - (Revenue and Profit impacts due to other marketing variables)

It should be clear from this why we can get such a different result when we choose to look only at Base Revenue and Profit and not take into account all of the other impacts that are occurring with a price promotion. It is also why many promotional events can appear to be profitable when they are not.

Let me give you a real example. At one time a common promotional event in the sanitary napkin category was a BOGO – Buy One Get One Free. Typically the consumer would be able to buy a large package of pads for $6.99 retail every week. During the promotion the consumer would be able to buy two packages for $6.99. The unit volume lift for this promotion was typically in the range of 200%. So, for example, if a retailer was selling 10,000 units per week with no promotion, the sales volume with a BOGO would be 30,000 units.

A basic analysis of this type of event would indicate that total revenue increased by about 50%. Base revenue would be 10,000 units times $6.99 or $69,900. Promotional revenue would be 30,000 units at $3.495 per unit or $104,850. The difference is about $34,950.

However, panel analysis showed that whenever consumers received a BOGO that the average household purchased 2.5 units during the promotional event. This analysis suggested that many consumers were stocking up during this event and we could reasonably assume that their future purchases were being affected. When we apply the pantry loading impact to the promotion we get a quite different result. In this case revenue would be equal to $87,375 minus the impact of pantry loading. The impact of pantry loading would be equal to 1.5 units sold at list price which is the amount of product that would be sold in the future if consumers did not stock up. In this case, that would be 15,000 units at a price of $6.99 or roughly $104,850.

From this analysis we would conclude that the actual impact of the promotional event on retail revenue was equal to a loss of $69,900. Armed with this type of analysis, one would conclude that this event was inefficient and non-productive.

Of course we can tie ourselves in knots trying to analyze every possible aspect of a pricing promotion. We seldom have all of the information or knowledge necessary to measure the impact precisely. And quite frankly I'm not sure it's possible to know exactly how much sales volume is pulled forward from the future or what future consumer behaviour will be like.

But that shouldn't be an excuse for not trying to get a better handle on the impact of promotional pricing. Even a rough estimate of the impact that takes into account how consumers behave when offered a price discount will be better than none at all.

☆ ☆ ☆

Avoiding Promotional Price Wars

Sometime in 2006 Proctor & Gamble decided to run a promotional event at Walgreen's where for every $10 purchased of a specific product the consumer received a $10 gift card from Walgreen's. The event drove a lot of sales which you might expect since it was the equivalent of getting the product for free. Not long after that, another competitor, Kimberley-Clark, started to run the same event at Walgreen's. By now it had spread beyond Walgreen's. That retailer's competitors, CVS and Rite-Aid, wanted to run the same event as well.

I can't speak for the success of this promotion for all competitors or for the retailers, but for at least one manufacturer it was nothing short of a disaster. The redemption rate on the gift cards was very high leading to a substantial promotional cost that far outweighed any benefits from additional sales volume. I have to believe that it was the same result for all manufacturers. Millions of dollars were spent achieving next to nothing.

The fact that so many competitors could waste so much money on a promotion is not surprising. Every time we run a promotional event we have some impact on our competitors and their behavior. Most promotional events are designed to have a negative impact on competitive sales volume. If that is the case, competitors will feel compelled to run their own promotional events to make up for the lost volume. Similarly, their events should have a negative impact on ours and ultimately we will feel compelled to respond in kind to make up for our lost volume.

Even if we don't have an impact, there is a competitive perception of pricing that will affect future promotions and how competitors try to leverage price and discounts to drive their market share. One of the reasons this happens is because we so often measure success in terms of market share. Whenever one competitor in a category runs a promotion their total sales and share will increase. Even if the sales volume for other competitors remains the same, their share will decrease because total sales volume has increased. Consequently, they will try to regain their 'share' through promotions.

Effective promotional pricing can have a deteriorating effect on category pricing overall if competitors engage in these types of price wars. In fact we can make an argument that truly effective promotional pricing that increases revenue and profit at competitors' expense will, in the long run, have negative consequences for everyone.

If that is the case, then the type of promotional pricing that we want to engage in is that which lifts category revenue and profit overall so that even when all competitors engage in promotional pricing there are benefits for everyone. This type of pricing is actually quite rare. It can happen in categories where there are a large number of consumers who will only enter the market when offered some sort of discount.

For our purposes, we should be mindful of both the category and the competitive impacts of promotional events and set a pricing strategy that does not encourage irresponsible competitive reactions.

We should also be aware of the impact that promotional pricing events have on retail customers. Retailers use promotional pricing to take business away from their competitors, who also happen to be your customers. Deep aggressive promotions with one customer will create demand from other customers for similar events. It can create a never ending spiral that reduces profit for everyone involved.

☆ ☆ ☆

What Does a Good Promotional Pricing Strategy Look Like?

All of the above would easily lead us to conclude that there is no such thing as a good promotional pricing strategy. If we have one that is effective in raising revenues and profits, it is likely to lead to promotional pricing wars. If we have one that is ineffective, we are just leaving money on the table. Either way we lose.

In an ideal world we would most likely do away with promotional events altogether, but unfortunately we don't live in such a place. If we start from the premise that promotional pricing is a necessary evil that we have to live with, then our objective in any pricing strategy is to minimize the damage that is created by that evil. To that extent, we need to do the following:

1. Identify the optimum volume lift for the retailer at the least cost to the manufacturer. Typically this should involve an ROI analysis to determine the effectiveness of trade spending.

2. Whenever possible use promotions that increase category revenue overall at the same time as they increase the sales of your own products. One of the best promotions I have seen is one that gave away a teddy bear around Valentine's day for the purchase of shampoo and conditioner. The gift was inexpensive, volume lift was substantial, and the cost was a lot less than having to give a discount. Since the store didn't sell teddy bears normally, there was no cannibalization of existing store sales.

3. Avoid excessive and deep discounts. These will lead to price wars and spur demand for even more discounting in the future.

4. Pay attention to price thresholds. We usually get the most bang for our buck by pricing just below a threshold. Any lower is just a waste of money.

5. Identify which SKUs have the best lift for the least cost and focus on these products.

6. Tie in promotional incentives to market objectives. Promote product sizes that you want to grow in total volume over time.

7. Use promotional pricing to encourage trial of new products. This type of promotional pricing satisfies retailers at the same time as it meets your marketing objectives.

Above all, you should constantly test new promotions and learn from your experience. Never assume that what you have in place is the best you can do. There are always new and better ways to increase the effectiveness of promotions and reduce the cost involved. On the other hand, it is an on-going battle just to avoid making promotional pricing disasters. Just doing that will probably mean that you are succeeding at least in part.

Case Study: KFC and the Beach Ball

Scott`s Chicken was a franchisee for KFC that owned a number of stories in Ontario, Canada. Among the many promotions that they ran each year, the one in August included a beach ball for every purchase of a bucket of chicken. The promotion was highly successful for a number of reasons.

The core KFC consumer who ate at KFC 2 or 3 times a week (at least at that time) bought the 2 piece chicken meal, with cole slaw, potato salad or fries. This represented almost 80% of their total business.

Buckets of chicken, however, were sold to a smaller segment of the market that was not a regular KFC customer. The Beach Ball Deal appealed to this non-regular segment of the market and had almost no impact on the core business. This is a standard characteristic of a good promotional event – lift without cannibalization of core sales.

Of course, KFC does not regularly sell beach balls so the giveaway had no impact on sales of chicken.

Another good feature of this promotion is that it tied in with an activity that was not usually associated with KFC – going to the beach with a bucket of chicken. Consumers were given an incentive to do something that they had not previously thought of doing. In this way, the promotion expanded the market for KFC into new territory.

Naturally any good promotion is based on the overall impact it has on revenues and profits. The beach ball promotion scored on both counts. Revenue lift was higher than for any other promotion the company offered.

In summary, the beach ball promotion was a success for the following reasons:

1. It focused on a market segment that was outside the core business.

2. It promoted a product that was low in volume and not part of the core product line.

3. It encouraged consumers to engage in an activity (taking KFC to the beach) that was outside their normal behaviour.

New Product Pricing

All of the concepts that we have discussed with respect to list prices are relevant to new product prices as swell. Value based pricing, portfolio pricing, competitive reaction, and so on are all elements of the new product pricing decision. At the same time there are some compelling differences with new product pricing that we need to consider.

Not all new product pricing decisions are difficult. Many new products fall into the 'me-too' category. They are either a variation on an existing product or a copy of something that is already in the market place. In either case, the price for the product will most likely be the same as an existing product or very close to it. At the same time, it is always good to ask whether or not a new product does have sufficient value to warrant a premium price relative to existing products. We make an error when we default too easily and line price new products with existing ones.

It is within the area of innovation that we find the biggest challenge for new product pricing. It is here where the value of the new product is sufficiently different from existing products that we have to consider a different price level.

In this chapter we will focus on three specific areas of new product pricing – using value based pricing within a new product pricing process, pricing research, and new product pricing strategy. Because we have already discussed these concepts, this section will focus on what is different or unique when dealing with new products.

✳ ✳ ✳

Using the Concept of Value to Determine New Product Features

Ideally, anytime we add value to a product or service through the addition of new features or improvements to existing features we should anticipate charging some higher price for that product or service. In a cost plus world we typically design the product first, determine the cost of production, then set the price to meet a profit margin hurdle. In a Value Based Pricing world we turn that process around. First, we determine what consumers value and what they are willing to pay for then decide how we can deliver that value in the most profitable fashion. This in turn drives the product development process.

When we use Value Based Pricing as the basis for setting prices we begin the process of new product development with the question of value and price. What value do different features bring to consumers? Which segments of the market will value these features? Are there elements of the innovation that have more value than others? Can we bundle or unbundle different elements of the new product based on what consumers` value? These questions should all be asked at the earliest stage of new product development.

From these questions we can begin the process of designing the new product or service with the goal in mind of creating the maximum value for consumers at the optimum price and margin for the manufacturer or service provider. We can eliminate ideas that are too costly or have low value for consumers, as well as direct the process towards finding answers that fit with consumer concepts of value.

This methodology is far superior to the process of creating something first then trying to decide what consumers will pay for it after the product has been developed. It reduces the risk of engaging in a lengthy product development cycle only to find at the end that the cost of production or delivery is far more than consumers are willing to pay. And it should almost always lead to a product or service design that is tailored to consumer wants with respect to both features and price.

☆ ☆ ☆

New Product Pricing Research

The emphasis on value driving product development implies some form of interaction with consumers to understand what they are willing to pay for. Typically this requires some market research.

There are several different methodologies that can be used to establish the price for a new product or service and most pricing research techniques that can be used for any list price can be used for new product pricing. The most common in use today are:

- Reference pricing
- Concept and price testing
- Van Westendorp
- Discrete Choice Analysis

Reference pricing for a new product consists of identifying an established product in the market place that consumers believe has the same value proposition as the new product. For example, suppose some inventive scientist developed a pill or vaccine that could prevent someone from catching the common cold (perhaps not that far away in reality). A reference product for this pill could be any similar preventative medicine that already exists, such as a flu vaccine, for example. The proposed price for the new product would be the same as that for the flu vaccine.

Reference pricing is obviously a very inexpensive methodology for new product pricing and that can make it very attractive. Nonetheless it has its weaknesses or flaws. It depends upon getting the right analogy with an existing product. This weakness can be overcome by some prudent consumer research to verify that consumers really do believe that the new product and the existing product have the same value proposition. It also assumes that the existing analogous product is priced correctly, not too low or too high. This weakness is more problematic and there is no way of knowing for certain that the price is optimal. Success in the marketplace for the existing product could be a sign of the right price or of a price that is too low. The third potential flaw in this methodology is that the analogy, although similar in the minds of consumers, might not be exact. Take our example of the cold vaccine and the use of a flu vaccine as a reference product. In reality, there are many competitive generic manufacturers of flu vaccines. But if the cold vaccine were patented and proprietary the pricing strategy and the right price for the new product could be quite different. Consumers might consider the two to be the same, but they would not take into account the value of the patent and the impact that would have on the pricing strategy.

Concept testing is a fairly limited and simple survey technique that asks respondents if they are likely to purchase or not at a specific price. This is not really a true pricing technique but it is very common. It might be useful if multiple prices were tested, but this would require a considerable number of tests to be run and that usually becomes expensive.

The applications for concept price testing are very limited. It is suitable for a situation where the new product is very similar to something already on the shelf (for example, a new flavor in an existing product), but aside from that it offers very little information. For the most part, it will confirm what we already know or expect to be the case.

Van Westendorp is a methodology that asks respondents to set a price for the new product or service based on four levels of value – basically, is it too cheap, not expensive yet, is beginning to get expensive, and is too expensive. The appropriate price for the new product is the intersection of the 'too cheap line' and the 'beginning to get expensive' lines when these are plotted on a graph. This typically represents the largest potential market share for the product or service.

Of course this assumes that the objective of the price you choose is to maximize market share for this particular product. That might not be the case if there are already products under the same brand in the category. That is one of the weaknesses of this methodology - it doesn't place the pricing question in context of the product portfolio.

Van Westendorp isn't designed to provide price elasticity or cross price elasticity with any other products. It won't tell you what might happen if you were to price the product higher or lower, or what impact different prices will have on the total portfolio of products within the brand that are currently on the shelf, i.e. other sizes, flavors, and so on. Because of this limitation, the most appropriate use for Van Westendorp is for a new product which is the only product that you have in your line up.

I have already discussed Discrete Choice Analysis in a previous chapter so I won't go into any more detail on that methodology in this section. It differs primarily from the other two in that it asks respondents to choose between the new product and existing products at various price levels. Within Discrete Choice we can also vary features and benefits. In some cases, it might be possible to test different features or concepts at different price levels in order to determine how each performs.

Of the three techniques, Discrete Choice is usually the more expensive but delivers the most in-depth understanding of the impact that price would have on the new product as well as the portfolio of existing products.

Choosing the appropriate methodology depends upon the product and the circumstances. The expense should be relative to the opportunity and the risk that is involved in the pricing decision. When choosing a pricing research methodology for a new product here are some of the questions you should ask:

1. Is this product significantly different from existing products?

2. Have we created new value that consumers will be willing to pay for?

3. What impact will this pricing decision have on future pricing decisions?

4. What is the risk if we under-price this product? If we over-price this product?

5. Can we adjust prices once the product has been launched?

6. How much investment are we willing to make to support the product launch?

7. Is this product part of a portfolio of products? Do we need to set the price relative to other products in the portfolio or can we price this product in isolation?

When we undertake any type of pricing research we should always keep in mind two key factors that will affect the outcome. These are:

1. allowing for survey error and
2. segmenting the survey.

Both can have a significant impact on how we interpret and use the results of the research as well as the findings that we achieve. Ultimately they will have an impact on the pricing decisions that we make.

✲ ✲ ✲

Survey Error

All surveys are subject to some sampling or survey error. The answer that we get from pricing research should never be taken as an absolute answer because there is some range within which the true answer might exist. Here is an example to illustrate this point.

I was once involved with pricing a new product where the pricing research had suggested that the correct retail list price for the product should be $23.99. This didn't seem to make a lot of sense since one would think that the price could just as well be $24.99. It is most likely that this is where the price threshold would exist, i.e. at $25. However, the market researcher was adamant that all the research pointed to $23.99. What she didn't consider was the possibility that, given the survey size, the range of possible prices could have been anywhere from $21.99 to $25.99 and that $23.99 just happened to be the result for this particular sample that was surveyed. As with all pricing research, we need to apply our own judgment to the findings.

Segmenting the Survey

When we are dealing with innovation market segmentation is critical. Not all consumers will place equal value on the innovation. It wouldn't make sense, for example, to ask someone in the market for an economy car how they would react to the price for a new Porsche.

In almost all cases those who value the innovation are likely to be willing to pay a higher price to get it than the rest of the market. When we survey the entire market, the answer that we get represents everyone's value. If, however, we focus on particular segments of the market, we can often get quite a different answer as to what the right price ought to be for that segment.

When designing a survey, therefore, it is important to identify which target markets the new product will be aimed at.

New Product Pricing Strategy

Many of the elements that go into new product pricing strategy are the same as those for existing products. These include market segments, the portfolio impact of prices, global markets, retailer impacts, competitive reaction and so on.

We touched on market segments above when discussing pricing research. The same principles that guide our research should be the basis of our pricing strategy. The price that we choose for the product should reflect what the target segment is willing to pay, not what the market as a whole wants to pay.

Any new product pricing should begin with an assessment of the impact that the product will have on overall revenue and profit for the portfolio of products. Too often we set new product prices in isolation and the price we choose, while it might be best for that product, is not necessarily the best price for the portfolio. This happens when we undervalue or under-price innovation and, as a result, we end up cannibalizing sales of existing products.

We should consider how competitors will react to the price that we set for this product. Launching a new product with superior features at the same price as a competitive product without those features can be considered nothing more than a price war. A competitor might have no alternative but to lower their price in order to maintain market share.

We should also view new product pricing from a retailer perspective. What will the price do for the retailer's category? We should remember that within any retail store there is a competition for shelf space. New products compete with existing products within the category, but the category also competes with other categories within the store. From a retailer's perspective a new product should increase the category's revenue and contribution as well as the store's total revenue and contribution. If we want to keep our retail customers happy and maintain or grow our competitive position within the category, we should pay attention to these impacts when we make pricing decisions.

Some of the key questions we should ask about new product prices are:

- How much volume do we need to maintain the product on the shelf? At what price will we achieve this volume?

- What is the cannibalization of existing product revenue and profit? At what price does this new product optimize overall revenue and profit?

- Does the retailer need the same margin as existing products, or will the margin for this new product be different?

- Will we use price promotions on this product? If so what will the promotional price be? How effective will this promotional price point be?

- How does the price of this product affect future new products that we intend to launch?

This last question is one that is worthy of some further discussion. We should always consider a new product pricing decision with an eye to the launch of future products. There are sometimes cases where a new product represents the first in a line of successive products that have some additional value for consumers. We need to price these products keeping in mind that the price we set will affect the price of future products in the same line. If we price the first one too low, then all subsequent launches will be priced lower as well.

✫ ✫ ✫

Towards Better Pricing

If you`ve made it this far, you should realize by now that pricing decisions are relatively complex affairs. Gut feel and intuition are poor substitutes for analysis and reason.

But a pricing decision requires more than just statistical analysis. Pricing analytics, strategic considerations, and scenario evaluation are just part of the pricing process. Just because we can analyze price elasticity does not mean that we have the right solution to a pricing problem.

Ultimately we start making better pricing decisions when we start asking the right questions. We need to recognize that there are always options and that each option will have a different impact on consumer and channel behavior. The optimal pricing position is one that searches for the right price relationship between our different products and those of the competition. As we change the product mix, the shelf design, features and benefits, that pricing relationship will change as well. We need to constantly re-assess the relationship and make adjustments.

Better pricing is always about challenging the status quo. Nothing about our world ever remains the same for long. Consumers change, retailers change, products change, economies change and so on, and with each change the impact that our prices have will change as well. We need to re-invent our approach to pricing to understand how the traditional practices and beliefs that have been instilled in our organization fit with a new marketing environment.

We should no longer accept unquestioningly the old norms of coupons, discounts, and other forms of price promotion. The impact that promotional pricing has on consumers will vary over time as market conditions, list prices, competitors, and retailers change. The spread of Every Day

Low Pricing strategies, dollar stores, internet channels and other types of low price shopping alternatives have lessened the impact that promotional pricing has on consumer behaviour and will continue to do so in the future.

As we venture into global markets, we should recognize that we need to develop pricing solutions that are suited towards each of these markets. Not all of these markets will behave in the same way that traditional markets have done in the past. Pricing relationships and promotional pricing strategies need to be set for each one in line with local conditions.

We need to recognize that all of our pricing decisions have a competitive impact. Using price as a weapon to gain market share in a mature market is the sort of strategy that can cause destructive competitive behaviour. We need to ask what impact a deep discount, higher rebates, or other forms of competitive pricing will have on the market and how a competitive pricing reaction will affect our own future revenues and profits before we engage in what could become a costly price war.

Better pricing seldom, if ever, happens overnight. It is a constant process that requires continual effort. If that sounds daunting, it shouldn't be. It simply means that pricing is something that we need to pay attention to just as we do to product development, advertising, distribution and other elements of marketing on an on-going basis.

The rewards are well worth the effort.

✧ ✧ ✧

Twenty Questions

1. Do prices for our products and services fit with the value offered relative to competition?

2. How well does our pricing strategy reflect and support our marketing strategy?

3. Can we articulate our pricing strategy?

4. How do we segment the market for pricing purposes?

5. Do consumers value added features and benefits?

6. Is there a segment of the market place that would pay a premium price for these features and benefits?

7. How does purchase behaviour affect consumption? If consumers buy more does the market grow?

8. Do we need to line price our products?

9. What is the appropriate pricing relationship between product sizes?

10. Are we offering package sizes that are at a package size threshold?

11. What would competitors do if we raised or lowered our prices?

12. Do we know how we will react to a change in competitive prices and what the impact will be?

13. What will retailers or distributors do if we change our prices?

14. What messages are we sending internally and externally about pricing?

15. What is the **net** impact of a pricing promotion on sales volume?

16. What would the impact be of fewer promotional events?

17. Do we have the right promotional price points and offers?

18. Do our promotional offers target the right products and market segments?

19. If we introduce a new promotional price what will the competitive reaction be?

20. Does our promotional strategy fit with our marketing strategy?

About the Author

Brian Wanless is a pricing specialist with more than 30 years' experience in marketing and pricing. He has spent the last 13 years working in the field of pricing. He was formerly Vice President of Pricing for the world's largest consumer healthcare products company and has been a pricing consultant to many Fortune 500 companies. He has written several articles on pricing and has been a guest speaker at pricing conferences and seminars throughout the world. He currently resides in Aurora, Ontario, Canada where he works as a pricing consultant.

He can be reached at bwanless@rogers.com.